HIGHER POWER

Doug Himes knows his Bible. He knows his Big Book. And he knows a multitude of quotations relevant to the way out. Here is an extremely well-written, scholarly formula for renewal. I loved reading it. And so will you.
—Dick B., author of 44 books and more than 1,000 articles on AA history and Christian recovery

Douglas Himes provides those who suffer from addictions with much inspiring and practical wisdom and guidance that can help them walk the ego self-emptying path that leads to the realization of their true self and life in God's image. His own 12-Step experience and considerable spiritual knowledge and practice enrich the value of his insights.
—Tilden Edwards, Founder and Senior Fellow, Shalem Institute for Spiritual Formation

Higher Power will guide and encourage all who are seeking recovery from addiction and all who are seeking "to live where it's real" in the spiritual life.
—Rt. Rev. Dr. William Wilson, Assisting Bishop, Anglican Diocese of the South - Director, Spiritual Life Ministry Foundation - Author, *Four Essentials: Classical Disciplines of Christian Spirituality*

Doug Himes has written a compelling resource, not only for those in recovery, but for all who struggle with their powerlessness over nouns of any kind. He makes a strong case for the importance and even necessity of the spiritual walk in recovery.
—William H. Swiggart, Co-Director, Center for Professional Health, Vanderbilt University Medical Center

I believe that this book can be equally read, understood, and experienced by those in 12-Step recovery and those with traditional faith-based backgrounds. My prayer is that the book will be a powerful tool for many "spiritual beings having a human experience."
—Ron Neufeld, licensed alcohol and drug counselor with more than 30 years of experience in addiction medicine

Higher Power captures the principles of the journey one must take to find God's love and healing for their suffering from alcohol or drug addiction. This spiritual quest of the person who is seeking sobriety, health, and wholeness must follow the principles outlined in this book.
—Anderson Spickard, Jr., M.D., Emeritus Professor of Medicine, Vanderbilt University Medical Center

HIGHER POWER

SEEKING GOD *in* 12-STEP RECOVERY

DOUGLAS D. HIMES

Abingdon Press / *Nashville*

HIGHER POWER
Seeking God in 12-Step Recovery

Copyright © 2012 by Douglas D. Himes

All rights reserved.

This book is printed on acid-free paper.

Library of Congress Cataloging-in-Publication Data

Himes, Douglas D., 1952-
  Higher power : seeking God in 12-step recovery / Douglas D. Himes.
    p. cm.
  ISBN 978-1-4267-4581-2 (book - pbk. / trade pbk. : alk. paper)   1.   Twelve-step programs—Religious aspects—Christianity. I. Title.
  BV4596.T88H56 2012
  248.8'629—dc23
                                                                    2012009185

Unpublished poem "What's the Problem?" © Victor Fried. Used by permission.

All Scripture quotations unless noted otherwise are taken from the New Revised Standard Version of the Bible, copyright 1989, Division of Christian Education of the National Council of the Churches of Christ in the United States of America. Used by permission. All rights reserved.

Abbreviations for books of the Bible conform to the standards established by the Society of Biblical Literature.

Scripture quotations noted KJV are from the King James or Authorized Version of the Bible.

Scripture quotations marked NIV are taken from the Holy Bible, NEW INTERNATIONAL READER'S VERSION®. Copyright © 1973, 1978, 1984 by International Bible Society. All rights reserved throughout the world. Used by permission of International Bible Society.

Scripture quotations marked REB are from the Revised English Bible © Oxford University Press and Cambridge University Press 1989.

"The Moses in my heart trembles" from SEASONS OF YOUR HEART: PRAYERS AND REFLECTIONS by MACRINA WIEDERKEHR. Copyright © 1991 by Macrina Wiederkehr. Reprinted by permission of HarperCollins Publishers.

Excerpts from four poems* from A TREE FULL OF ANGELS by MACRINA WIEDERKEHR. Copyright © 1988 by Macrina Wiederkehr. Reprinted by permission of HarperCollins Publishers.

*"A Magnificant for Coming Home" (14 lines excerpted): "For your prayer" (18): "Alone" (8): "The quiet in me smiled on my noise" (19)

12 13 14 15 16 17 18 19 20 21—10 9 8 7 6 5 4 3 2 1

MANUFACTURED IN THE UNITED STATES OF AMERICA

In memory of
John Ishee
(1934–2012)

friend, mentor, and colleague

whose spiritual counsel
gave life to countless recovering
alcoholics and addicts

and

whose healing spirit lives on
in these pages

CONTENTS

PREFACE

The early twentieth-century French Jesuit mystic Pierre Teilhard de Chardin wrote: "We are not human beings having a spiritual experience; we are spiritual beings having a human experience." Our spirituality is not something that we have to look for, nor is it something that we put on and take off like a garment. Our spirituality is our very essence, at the core of our being, beneath all of the human stuff. Spiritual growth is a totally natural process; but it is also absolutely essential to anyone wishing to recover from anything. A close reading of the fundamental text *Alcoholics Anonymous*, commonly referred to as the "Big Book," reveals the grave reality that, for every recovering alcoholic or addict, there will come a time when the only thing that stands between that person and picking up a drink or drug will be the person's relationship with his or her Higher Power. When I reach that point, it will not matter how many treatment programs I've been through, how many sponsors or sponsees I've had, how many meetings I've attended, or how much of the Big Book I can recite from memory. The only thing that will prevent my picking up a drink or drug will be my personal relationship with my Higher Power. This is the part of the Program that I absolutely must get, for it is this part of the Program, more than any other, that will keep me alive.

The Big Book describes alcoholism as an "illness that only a spiritual experience will conquer."[1] This book is an invitation into that spiritual experience. Although its chapters follow the progression from darkness into light generally experienced by anyone who consents to the miracle of recovery in his or her life, the chapters can be read in any order, according to the needs of the reader. Each chapter offers a meditation on some aspect of recovery that I have found important in my own journey from darkness into light. And every chapter is based on one or more passages of Scripture from the Judeo-Christian tradition, which served as the foundation for the philosophy of Alcoholics Anonymous and other 12-Step Programs. If you are in recovery and gazing into the chasm between spirituality and organized religion that has evolved in the recovery community, this book will offer you a bridge over that chasm. The book also extends a twofold invitation:

1. to move gently, at your own pace, into an ever-deepening personal relationship with a Higher Power, healing any preconditioned image of God that may stand in your way;
2. to enter your fundamental essence, your spiritual core, that place of total authenticity where you can be one with the God of your understanding, and out of which you can live a life that is genuine and serene.

Come with me as I look at some significant benchmarks in the journey of recovery. Walk with me through parts of my story and marvel at how much of your own story can be found here, as well.

—⁓— —⁓— —⁓—

As the fog began to lift, and my life slowly came into focus, I didn't fully understand how I had gotten there. Ten months earlier, I had moved to Nashville to marry for the second time and spend the rest of my life in contented prosperity. In less than a year of advanced active addiction, I had destroyed that relationship (actually, alcoholics don't have relationships, they take hostages), and I hit bottom.

I checked myself into Cumberland Heights, one of the country's leading alcohol and drug treatment centers, which "happens" to be located in Nashville. (I now understand that God had carefully engineered all of this, but I certainly did not know that at the time.) It had been nine and a half years since my first encounter with Alcoholics Anonymous and addiction counseling—a year and a half spent as a "dry drunk," followed by eight years of additional "field work."

I had finally reached that point familiar to most people in recovery, where my life was falling apart faster than I could lower my standards. I had never known such excruciating pain, and I was willing to do anything anyone told me to do, if it would just stop the hurt. After nine and a half years, I finally got honest enough to embrace the First Step, admitting that I was powerless over alcohol, and that my life—what was left of it—had become unmanageable. As I began to work my way through the succeeding Steps, the miracle of recovery started to unfold in my life.

Almost immediately following treatment, I was led in two directions. First, I discerned a clear call to a ministry in spiritual direction, in which I was subsequently trained, and in which I remain deeply involved. The second direction became clear in an invitation to assist with chapel worship at Cumberland Heights—at first, leading music, and later as Chaplain Assistant, in which role I was called upon also occasionally to preach, lecture, and lead worship and workshops.

By the time I reached recovery, my hunger for spiritual nourishment was so acute that I read forty-five books on spirituality during the first year of my sobriety. Among the many inspirational and helpful works that I devoured, the most breathtaking was a book entitled *A Tree Full of Angels* by the Benedictine sister Macrina Wiederkehr, a modest volume that encourages us to be aware of the holiness that surrounds us, and to be attentive to the movement of God in all aspects of our life.[2] As we find so often with AA and other 12-Step meetings, it offered "just what I needed to hear." In recognition of the extent to which Sister Macrina's wisdom shaped my early sobriety, I have quoted liberally from her prose and poetry, in hopes that her thoughts and prayers may feed your soul as profoundly as they have fed mine.

When I first got sober, I thought that my problem was alcohol—and alcoholism. I soon learned from veterans in the Program that alcohol and drugs were never our problem; they were our *solution*. Our problem was an inability to live life on life's terms, and we used alcohol and drugs to medicate the pain caused by that inability.

The solution to our problem, 12-Step recovery, is also not about alcohol, or drugs, or addiction. Twelve-Step recovery is about life. Alcohol is mentioned only once in the Twelve Steps, in the first half of the First Step. From that point onward, everything is about life and universal truth. There is no principle in the Twelve Steps of Alcoholics Anonymous that has not been around for thousands of years. AA cofounder Bill Wilson's primary contribution was that he wrote them down and numbered them, so that we could work them in order. Twelve-Step recovery works, because it treats all of life, not merely an isolated disease. The Twelve Steps offer anyone, whether addicted or not, one of the most successful models for spiritual growth and healing ever devised. The ultimate goal of the Steps is "conscious contact with God"—for anyone.

It has been said that the best way for a person of faith to navigate recovery is with a copy of the Big Book in one hand and a copy of the Bible in the other. Speaking about the role of the Bible in the early years of Alcoholics Anonymous, AA cofounder Dr. Bob Smith stated: "We were convinced that the answer to our problems was in the Good Book."[3] That remains true today. For that reason, I have included throughout the text citations for references to or quotations from Scripture, as an invitation to explore this valuable resource, or perhaps to reconnect with stories familiar from an earlier time in life. Occasionally I have included a brief explanation of a scriptural reference, exploring it more fully for a deeper comprehension of its relevance for recovery. With one foot firmly planted in the universal truth of the Big Book and the other foot firmly planted in the universal truth of the Good Book, you can live a balanced life at peace with yourself and the rest of God's Creation.

While drawn from my personal experience in addiction and recovery, this book is about life. Any insights contained in these pages were given to me by God, as God has shaped my understanding both of the spiritual life and of God's desire that we should "have life, and have it abundantly" (John 10:10b). I am deeply grateful for the countless people through whom God has channeled wisdom—from fellow sojourners in the rooms of Alcoholics Anonymous to the thousands of patients and residents in various treatment centers in whose early recovery I have been blessed to participate. Most of what you read in this book was taught to me. I pass it along to you to pass along to others, with the firm conviction that, in the world of 12-Step recovery, if we don't *carry* the message, we won't *get* the message.

And just as others have been transparent to God's message for my life, I pray that I, too, may be transparent to God's message for your life. May these reflections serve as a window through which you may glimpse the shimmerings of a better way, and see more clearly the path that God has set before you and the fullness of life to which he is inviting you.

A Prayer in the Darkness

Most merciful and loving God, it can be so dark where we are. At those times in our lives when we close our eyes, and all we feel is pain; when we open our eyes, and all we see is darkness; help us to reach out into the darkness, to take the hand that has been extended to us since the moment of our birth, that we may walk hand in hand, step by step, with you, the One who calls us out of darkness into your marvelous light. Amen.

ONE

DO YOU WANT TO
BE MADE WELL?

*N*ow in Jerusalem by the Sheep Gate there is a pool, called
in Hebrew Beth-zatha, which has five porticoes. In these
lay many invalids—blind, lame, and paralyzed. One man was
there who had been ill for thirty-eight years. When Jesus saw him
lying there and knew that he had been there a long time, he said
to him, "Do you want to be made well?" The sick man answered
him, "Sir, I have no one to put me into the pool when the water
is stirred up; and while I am making my way, someone else steps
down ahead of me." Jesus said to him, "Stand up, take your mat
and walk." At once the man was made well, and he took up his
mat and began to walk.

—John 5:2-9a

The miracle of recovery contains a paradox: one must consent
to the miracle in order to participate in it. This chapter poses the
question whose answer is the gateway to the miracle.

━〜━ ━〜━ ━〜━

It seems a strange question: "Do you want to be made well?"
The man in John's Gospel had been paralyzed for thirty-eight

years. He was sick, miserable, helpless, pitiful. Why wouldn't he want to be made well? Why wouldn't *anyone* who had been sick that long want to be made well?

Located in northeast Jerusalem, the pool in the story is actually two pools surrounded and separated by five porticoes, or covered porches. According to a combination of ancient folklore and Jewish superstition, it was believed that an angel of the Lord went down at certain seasons into the pool and stirred up the water. Whoever stepped in first, after the stirring of the water, was made well from whatever disease that person had. As a result of this belief, the five porticoes were filled with invalids—sick people with all manner of diseases and disabilities—waiting for the stirring of the waters and hoping then to be the first into the pool. It was into this gathering of broken humanity that Jesus walked.

The Gospel tells us that the central character of the story is a man who has been paralyzed for thirty-eight years. He has come to this pool—perhaps every day for thirty-eight years—hoping to be magically healed by the stirred waters. Every time he struggles to drag himself to the waters, someone beats him to it; and, defeated once again, he returns to his pallet. (If this happened just once a day for thirty-eight years, he would have made nearly fourteen thousand attempts to reach the pool!) Life for him was a saga of perpetual hopelessness.

COMFORTABLE HOPELESSNESS

There is, however, a certain comfortable familiarity in his hopelessness. While able men toil and sweat all day in the blazing sun, the paralyzed man sits in the shade of the portico. People who see him feel sorry for him. They undoubtedly bring him things and do things for him, compensating for his disability; and no one expects anything from him. Each day is characterized by a numbing sameness. There is predictable comfort in his hopelessness.

There is comfort in our hopelessness as well. Like Saint Augustine in the fourth century, we find again and again—often to our bewilderment—that the life to which we are accustomed grips us more firmly than the life for which we long. An Arab chief tells the story of a spy captured and sentenced to death by a general in the Persian army. This general had the strange custom of giving condemned criminals a choice between the firing squad and "the big, black door." The moment for the execution

The best opportunities in our lives stand behind the forbidding door of the great unknown.

drew near, and guards brought the spy to the Persian general.

"What will it be," asked the general, "the firing squad or 'the big, black door'?"

The spy hesitated for a long time. Finally he chose the firing squad.

A few minutes later, hearing the shots ring out confirming the spy's execution, the general turned to his aide and said: "They always prefer the known to the unknown. People fear what they don't know. Yet, we gave him a choice."

"What lies beyond the big door?" asked the aide.

"Freedom," replied the general. "I've known only a few brave enough to take that door."

The best opportunities in our lives stand behind the forbidding door of the great unknown. We are more comfortable, however, with "the devil we know" than with any risk of change, even if it would mean a better life. We become resigned to our own disabilities.

Like the paralytic in the Gospel story, we, too, spend a great deal of time sitting on our mat, paralyzed, beside various pools in this life where we hope somehow to be cured. We feel sorry for ourselves, attributing our disabled state to a variety of insufficiencies: we're not strong enough, smart enough, rich enough, attractive enough, popular enough. We blame others for not helping us into the pool. We resent those who step in front of us and get what we think we deserve. In all of this we cling stubbornly to our illusion that what we *do* can in any way bring about our healing. We seek magic where only a miracle will suffice.

In Alcoholics Anonymous, we enter recovery through the first three Steps, which we summarize by the qualities that they require of us: Honesty, Openness, Willingness. It's *H-O-W* we get into recovery. The Big Book calls these qualities "indispensable," "the essentials of recovery."[1] Phrases like "Surrender to Win" and "Let Go and Let God" become mantras that sustain us in our sobriety one day at a time. In "How It Works," the passage from the Big Book that has been read at the beginning of AA meetings since 1950, we are reminded that "some of us have tried to hold on to our old ideas and the result was nil until we let go absolutely."[2] We must let go absolutely, if we are to experience *release*. We must let go of our own controlling, in order to let God do what only God can do to heal our brokenness.

THE PARADOX OF SURRENDER

This key point is explained further by authors Ernest Kurtz and Katherine Ketcham in their marvelous book *The Spirituality of Imperfection*:

> Alcoholism and addiction, characterized as they are by the rigid clinging of obsession and compulsion, help us to understand the experience of release. Perhaps the greatest paradox in the story of spirituality is the mystical insight that we are able to experience release only if we ourselves *let go*. This is the paradox of *surrender*. Surrender begins with the acceptance that we are not in control of the matter at hand—in fact, we are not in absolute control of anything. Thus the experience of surrender involves the "letting in" of reality that becomes possible when we are ready to let go of our illusions and pretensions (our "unreality").[3]

A familiar poem expresses it poignantly:

> As children bring their broken toys
> With tears for us to mend,
> I brought my broken dreams to God,
> Because he was my friend.

But then instead of leaving him
In peace to work alone,
I hung around and tried to help
With ways that were my own.

At last I snatched them back and cried,
"How can you be so slow?"
"My child," he said, "what could I do?
You never did let go."

As in the Third Step, in which we make a decision to turn our will and our lives over to the care of God as we understand God, surrender is an integral part of faith. Surrender is not an abandonment of ourselves in the face of difficulty, nor is it synonymous with submission. We yield ourselves to God freely, not under coercion. Surrender is not resignation, but rather an *invitation* into something greater, fuller than ourselves. It is an invitation to be ourselves more fully. Surrender is not so much *giving* up as it is an *opening* up. We open ourselves to new perspectives and dimensions of life yet to be explored. Through surrender we are brought more fully into ourselves and, at the same time, into that fullness which is greater than all that is. As discussed more fully in chapter 15, surrender is an absolute requirement for recovery.

Surrender is an integral part of faith.

Many of us have been able to experience release and surrender only when we reached a point of exhaustion where we were

willing to let go of our own efforts and permit ourselves simply to
be. The nineteenth-century American evangelist Dwight L.
Moody related a story told to him by a friend:

> Dr. Andrew Boar told me how, in the highlands of Scotland,
> sheep would often wander off into the rocks and get into places
> that they couldn't get out of. The grass on these mountains is
> very sweet, and the sheep will jump down ten or twelve feet,
> and can't jump back again. They may be there for days, until
> they have eaten all the grass.
>
> The shepherd will wait until they are so faint they cannot
> stand, and then he will put a rope around himself and go over
> and pull the sheep up out of the jaws of death.
>
> "Why doesn't he go down there when the sheep first get
> there?" I asked.
>
> "Ah," Dr. Boar said, "if he did, the sheep are so very foolish
> they would dash right over the precipice and be killed!"

How true that is for so many of us who resist recovery right up
to the point where we are finally too exhausted to hurl our self
over the precipice to our own death.

Once we have decided in the Third Step to turn our will
and our lives over to the care of the God of our understanding, we are led in due time to the Sixth Step, where we
become entirely ready to have God remove all of our defects
of character. This is the heart of the message. It is God who
removes our defects of character; it is *only* God who can heal
us. Healing is a miracle. It is not anything we can do for ourselves. Like the grace of God, we do not deserve it and cannot
possibly earn it. It is freely given to us. We have only to accept

it. And this brings us back to Bethzatha. Come along with me to that place.

The air is hot and dry, laden with dust from the nearby road. You can feel the dryness on your skin, see the clouds of dust floating by. You can hear and smell the sheep as they are driven through the nearby gate in the wall encircling the city, on their way to sale in the market or sacrifice in the temple. As you sit by the pool on your mat, resigned to your paralysis, a stranger approaches.

Surrender . . . is an invitation to be ourselves more fully.

Standing before you, the stranger looks deeply into your eyes. It feels as if he can see right to the bottom of your soul. He knows that you, like the paralytic in the Gospel, have been here a long time. He speaks to you, reaching the deepest places of your brokenness. You can see in his eyes that the question he poses is not rhetorical. He does not say: "Wouldn't you like to be better off than you are now?" But rather: "Are you willing to let go of your comfortable hopelessness? Are you willing to give up the excuses that you use to justify your disability? Are you willing to have removed those defects of character that keep you from wholeness? Are you willing to open your hands and your heart to receive this unconditional, lifesaving gift?"

And you hear the tender words: *"Do you want to be made well?"*

How will you answer?

TWO

FINDING OUR WAY OUT OF THE DARKNESS

*B*lessed be the God and Father of our Lord Jesus Christ! By
his great mercy he has given us a new birth into a living
hope through the resurrection of Jesus Christ from the dead, and
into an inheritance that is imperishable, undefiled, and unfading,
kept in heaven for you, who are being protected by the power of
God through faith for a salvation ready to be revealed in the last
time. In this you rejoice, even if now for a little while you have
had to suffer various trials, so that the genuineness of your
faith—being more precious than gold that, though perishable, is
tested by fire—may be found to result in praise and glory and
honor when Jesus Christ is revealed. Although you have not seen
him, you love him; and even though you do not see him now, you
believe in him and rejoice with an indescribable and glorious joy,
for you are receiving the outcome of your faith, the salvation of
your souls.

—1 Peter 1:3-9

By the time we reach recovery, our losses can be extensive,
leaving us to face a mountain of grief in a very dark place. How
do we find our way out of that place? Is there any way to avoid
the pain? Why is this happening to us?

She lay so still. How small and frail she seemed. Just eighteen months ago she had been a beautiful, talented second-grader, full of life and energy—a violin recital and a dance recital in the same day! Then suddenly the illness and the diagnosis: acute leukemia. Eighteen months of excruciating pain, treatment, remission, more pain, more treatment. Through countless hours he had knelt by her bed, holding her small hand, praying that somehow she would be spared. Now he had watched her take her last breath, as she departed alone on a journey that he could not comprehend. *Why, God, why? What did we do to deserve this? What purpose could possibly be served by the death of a ten-year-old girl in a loving Christian family? Where are you, God, in this overwhelming pain?*

Her name was Laura Lue Claypool. Her father, John, was a pastor and one of the great spiritual writers of our time.[1] I suspect that most of us have been where he was. We may not have lost a child; for us perhaps it was a parent, or other loved one, or a close relationship. Many of us lost our life in our addiction. At some point, we find our self plunged into a darkness that seems to go on forever, alone in a wilderness of pain and despair. What do we understand about that place? How do we survive it? Where is God in our darkness?

Suffering is not only a part of life; it is an essential and vitally important part of life. Buddha taught Four Noble Truths, the first of which was: Life is suffering. Suffering is universal. No one is immune from it. Even Jesus, who was as human as we are, experienced overwhelming desperation and abandonment when he cried out on the cross: "My God, my God, why have you forsaken me?" (Matt 27:46b).

Anyone who has struggled with addiction has certainly known suffering, perhaps as a constant companion for many years. Hitting bottom in my own addiction, I became engulfed by a world of pain I had never before experienced. For the first time, I understood what the psalmist described as "the valley of the shadow of death." I could sleep for no more than four hours at a time before waking up to begin crying again. Many days I could barely function. Some days it was almost literally impossible to put one foot in front of the other to walk. I existed under the constant, crushing weight of grief, separated from all of my hopes and dreams. My pain seemed larger than life itself. I wanted to scream with the psalmist: "Out of the depths I cry to you, O LORD. Lord, hear my voice!" (Ps 130:1, 2). I felt totally abandoned.

Many great figures throughout history have experienced and documented such suffering. You may recall the movie *Shadowlands*, which tells the story of how the great twentieth-century Christian apologist C. S. Lewis, a confirmed bachelor, found himself, at the age of fifty-six, married to Joy Davidman and stepfather to her two children. After only four years of glorious happiness together, Joy died of cancer, and Lewis chronicled in several journals the devastating grief that tested his faith. From the depths of his despair he wrote:

> Meanwhile, where is God? This is one of the most disquieting symptoms. When you are happy, so happy that you have no sense of needing Him, if you turn to Him then with praise, you

will be welcomed with open arms. But go to Him when your need is desperate, when all other help is vain and what do you find? A door slammed in your face, and a sound of bolting and double bolting on the inside. After that, silence. You may as well turn away.[2]

We can learn a great deal in the darkness of our suffering. I'd like to suggest four valuable insights that I believe we can find in our pain.

The first insight is: God did not cause our suffering. In the throes of despair we are tempted to question why God would want to hurt us so deeply. We are asking the wrong question, often arising from an image, perhaps conditioned from our youth, of a vengeful, punishing God of wrath—a "gotcha God." God does not want us to suffer, and God does not cause our suffering. Because God has *allowed* something to happen does not mean that God has *willed* it to happen. When God created the universe, God built into it two fundamental principles: a physical world that runs according to consistent natural laws, and human freedom. God will never interfere with either, for to do so would be to violate God's own gift. Living life on life's terms requires that we come to grips with this reality. We cannot change the laws of nature; and human freedom, in the hands of one who does not know how to use it, can be a deadly weapon. In the Hebrew

> *Because God has allowed something to happen does not mean that God has willed it to happen.*

Wisdom Literature, we read: "Whoever digs a pit will fall into it, and a stone will come back on the one who starts it rolling" (Prov 26:27). It is one of the overarching principles of the Hebrew Bible/Old Testament: Wrong choices lead to painful consequences. How many times have we proven that in our lives? It's not God's fault. In some ways it would be easier for God to step in, to have faith *for* us, to help us in extraordinary ways; but God has instead chosen to stand before us, arms extended, while encouraging *us* to walk, to participate in the development of our own soul. That process always involves struggle, and often involves suffering.

IN OUR PAIN LIES GREAT PROMISE

The second insight that I believe we can find in our suffering is: in our pain lies great promise. The psalmist wrote: "Weeping may linger for the night, but joy comes with the morning" (Ps 30:5b). "Those who sow in tears reap with shouts of joy" (Ps 126:5). The purpose of suffering is not the suffering itself. If we think it's about the pain, we have missed the point. The question central to all suffering is not the backward-looking "Why?" but rather the forward-looking "To what end?" It is of the

Faith means believing in advance what will only make sense in reverse.

essence of God's grace that God cares much more about the person we can become than about the person we have been. The apostle

Paul wrote in his letter to the Romans: "We also boast in our sufferings, knowing that suffering produces endurance, and endurance produces character, and character produces hope" (Rom 5:3, 4). In the Epistle of James we read: "My brothers and sisters, whenever you face trials of any kind, consider it nothing but joy, because you know that the testing of your faith produces endurance; and let endurance have its full effect, so that you may be mature and complete, lacking in nothing" (Jas 1:2-4). To the Romans Paul wrote further: "I consider that the sufferings of this present time are not worth comparing with the glory about to be revealed to us" (Rom 8:18). The pain of life is not about the sufferings of the present time; it is about the glory about to be revealed. The prophet Jeremiah wrote: "For surely I know the plans I have for you, says the LORD, plans for your welfare and not for harm, to give you a future with hope" (Jer 29:11-13). Our faith is grounded in that hope, for faith means believing in advance what will only make sense in reverse.

The question central to all suffering is not the backward-looking "Why?" but rather the forward-looking "To what end?"

THE STONECUTTER'S CHISEL

Roman Catholic priest and spiritual writer Henri Nouwen often related a story that illuminated his own suffering:

I once saw a stonecutter remove great pieces from a huge rock on which he was working. In my imagination I thought, *That rock must be hurting terribly. Why does this man wound the rock so much?* But as I looked longer, I saw the figure of a graceful dancer emerge gradually from the stone, looking at me in my mind's eye and saying, "You foolish man, didn't you know that I had to suffer and thus enter into my glory?"[3]

Nouwen realized that what appeared to be a brutal process of tearing down was actually a creative process of removing whatever was obscuring the beauty that lay beneath.

Dr. Martin Luther King, Jr., knew suffering not only in his own life but also in an entire race. Building on a quotation from the nineteenth-century German philosopher Friedrich Nietzsche, he said: "What doesn't destroy me makes me stronger." Amplifying Jesus' requirement of his followers that they "take up their cross daily and follow me" (Luke 9:23), Dr. King asserted that it is the marks of that cross on us that redeem us to a more excellent way that comes only through suffering.[4]

THE REFINER'S FIRE

I remember in my early recovery, as I began to grasp the work that lay ahead, coming to the realization that my life had become a kind of crucible, a vessel in which precious metal is refined by burning away its impurities under intense heat. Suddenly all of the furnace references in the Bible made sense:

- "The promises of the LORD are promises that are pure, silver refined in a furnace on the ground, purified seven times" (Ps 12:6).
- "Like gold in the furnace he tried them" (Wis 3:6a).
- "For he is like a refiner's fire . . . he will sit as a refiner and purifier of silver . . ." (Mal 3:2b, 3).

When her women's Bible study group encountered the latter passage with some curiosity, one member decided to investigate the process described in the Bible verse and went to visit a silversmith.

We are being refined until God can see God's image in us.

"Sir," she asked him, "do you sit while the work of refining is going on?"

"Oh, yes, ma'am," replied the silversmith, "I have to sit and watch the furnace constantly, because if the time necessary for refining is exceeded in the slightest degree, the silver will be injured."

Before she left, the lady asked one final question: "How do you know when the process is complete?"

"That's quite simple," replied the silversmith. "When I can see my own image in the silver, the refining process is finished."

This is what happens to us in the crucible of our lives. We are being refined until God can see God's image in us. This is the great promise in our pain, the living hope in our darkness.

WE ARE NEVER ALONE

The third insight to be found in our suffering is this: We are never alone in the darkness. The eminent twentieth-century Jewish theologian Martin Buber maintained that the Hebrew text recording God's self-revelation to Moses on Mount Sinai as "I AM WHO I AM" (Exod 3:14) can be translated more accurately as "I SHALL BE THERE AS I SHALL BE THERE." It is the central message of the Christmas story. It is why the Messiah was called "Emmanuel," which means "God is with us." No matter how deep our darkness, we will never be alone. God is with us.

God's constant presence in our darkness can be illustrated by the story of a young man whose wife died, leaving him with a small son. After returning from the cemetery, they went to bed as soon as it was dark, because there

No matter how deep our darkness, we will never be alone. God is with us.

was nothing else the father could bear to do. As he lay there in the darkness—brokenhearted, grief-stricken, numb with sorrow—from his bed across the room, the little boy broke the stillness: "Where is Mommy?" The father tried to get the boy to go to sleep, but the questions kept coming. After a while, the father got up and brought the boy to bed with him; but the child was still disturbed and restless. Finally, the boy reached out in the darkness and placed his hand on his father's face, asking: "Is your face toward me? If your face is toward me, I think I can go to sleep."

Assured, in a little while the boy grew quiet. The path from active addiction to recovery involves much time spent in the darkness asking agonizing questions. We can find peace in the assurance that God's face is always toward us. We have only to turn ourselves toward him to connect with our Higher Power.

LIGHT IN OUR DARKNESS

The final insight contains great hope: There is light in our darkness. A member of my AA home group recalls the point in his early recovery when he saw within himself the first spark of his comprehension of sobriety. As he describes it, the spark ignited a small flame, and it is that flame that he nurtures every day by working the Program. Each of us in recovery has within us our own flame, which we, too, must nurture. It illuminates not only *our* life, but also the lives of those around us. It is God's light shining within us. It is not a searchlight that beams far into the distance, illuminating the future. God's light is a lamp that gives us only light enough to take the next few steps—and that's all we need.

Beginning with the description of the Creation, when God's light pierced the darkness that "covered the face of the deep" (Gen 1:1-5), images of God's light/lamp have shone throughout both Hebrew and Christian Scripture:

- "It is you who light my lamp; the LORD, my God, lights up my darkness" (Ps 18:28).

- "Your word is a lamp to my feet and a light to my path" (Ps 119:105).

- "Where can I go from your spirit? Or where can I flee from your presence? . . . If I say, 'Surely the darkness shall cover me, and the light around me become night,' even the darkness is not dark to you; the night is as bright as the day, for darkness is as light to you" (Ps 139:7, 11, 12).

- "The people who walked in darkness have seen a great light; those who lived in a land of deep darkness—on them light has shined" (Isa 9:2).

- "What has come into being in him was life, and the life was the light of all people. The light shines in the darkness, and the darkness did not overcome it" (John 1:3b-5).

Jesus once referred to his forerunner, John the Baptist, as "a burning and shining lamp" (John 5:35). He also referred to himself in terms of light:

- "I am the light of the world. Whoever follows me will never walk in darkness but will have the light of life" (John 8:12).

- "The light is with you for a little longer. Walk while you have the light, so that the darkness may not overtake you. If you walk in the darkness, you do not know where you are going. While you have the light, believe in the light, so that you may become children of light. . . . I have come as light into the world, so that everyone who believes in me should not remain in the darkness" (John 12:35, 36a, 46).

Light is also an important image in the literature of Alcoholics Anonymous. The Big Book refers to God as "the Father of Light who presides over us all."[5] In the instructive commentary of the companion volume to the Big Book, *Twelve Steps and Twelve Traditions* (12 X 12), light figures prominently. With regard to the "searching and fearless moral inventory of ourselves" prescribed in Step Four, the 12 X 12 notes that one of the goals of assisting newcomers to the Program in sweeping the "*searchlight* of Step Four" back and forth over their lives is "to help them discover a chink in the walls their ego has built, through which the *light* of reason can shine."[6] Of the Fourth Step, the 12 X 12 says further: "Once we have a complete willingness to take inventory, and exert ourselves to do the job thoroughly, a wonderful *light* falls on this foggy scene."[7] With regard to Step Eleven, the 12 X 12 asserts: "We all need the *light* of God's reality, the nourishment of His strength, and the atmosphere of His grace."[8] In working our Twelfth Step, the 12 X 12 notes that one of the things "we receive as we carry A.A.'s message to the next alcoholic" is "to watch the eyes of men and women open with wonder as they move from darkness into *light*."[9] [my italics throughout] Every one of us in addiction yearns desperately to experience that wonder as we "move from darkness into light."

LEAVING THE DARKNESS BEHIND

Active addiction is a condition of progressive, personal darkness. By the time we hit bottom, we are enshrouded by that darkness; it stretches in every direction as far as we can see. Look for the light in the darkness of your suffering. It is there. Both John Claypool and C. S. Lewis found light in the depths of their personal darkness. The light that pierced the darkness of their suffering was the realization that the precious daughter and beloved wife whose losses they mourned were nothing less than pure gifts from God, changing and enriching and enlightening their lives forever, beyond physical death. The light in our darkness is the Program of Alcoholics Anonymous delivered by the hand of a loving God who has the power to overcome any darkness and lead us to safety. With God's face turned toward us, and God's hand to guide us, we can walk confidently out of any darkness toward our Higher Power.

THREE

CHOOSE LIFE

*H*appy are those
       who do not follow the advice of the wicked,
or take the path that sinners tread,
    or sit in the seat of scoffers;
but their delight is in the law of the LORD,
    and on his law they meditate day and night.
They are like trees
    planted by streams of water,
which yield their fruit in its season,
    and their leaves do not wither.
In all that they do, they prosper.

The wicked are not so,
    but are like chaff that the wind drives away.
Therefore the wicked will not stand in the judgment,
    nor sinners in the congregation of the righteous;
for the LORD *watches over the way of the righteous,*
    but the way of the wicked will perish.

                                            —Psalm 1

*S*ee, I have set before you today life and prosperity, death and
    adversity. If you obey the commandments of the LORD your
God that I am commanding you today, by loving the LORD your

*God, walking in his ways, and observing his commandments,
decrees, and ordinances, then you shall live and become numerous, and the* LORD *your God will bless you in the land that you
are entering to possess. But if your heart turns away and you do
not hear, but are led astray to bow down to other gods and serve
them, I declare to you today that you shall perish; you shall not
live long in the land that you are crossing the Jordan to enter and
possess. I call heaven and earth to witness against you today that
I have set before you life and death, blessings and curses. Choose
life so that you and your descendants may live, loving the* LORD
*your God, obeying him, and holding fast to him; for that means
life to you and length of days, so that you may live in the land
that the* LORD *swore to give to your ancestors, to Abraham, to
Isaac, and to Jacob.*

—Deuteronomy 30:15-20

Addiction robs us of choices. Recovery gives us a new life filled
with choices. To choose recovery over active addiction is to
choose life over death. It is an ancient choice that takes on powerful relevance for anyone making the transition from active
addiction to recovery.

—w— —w— —w—

In May 2003, a twenty-seven-year-old hiker named Aron
Ralston was climbing in a remote canyon in southeastern Utah,
when an eight-hundred-pound boulder fell on him, pinning his
right arm to the ground. All efforts to free himself proved futile.

After three days, he ran out of water. After five days, he realized that he was going to die under the boulder unless he took drastic action. He managed to break both bones in his lower arm and then used a dull pocket knife to amputate the limb below the elbow. After applying a tourniquet and administering first aid, he rappelled to the canyon floor below, where he was later rescued. Choosing life over death can be painful. Anyone who has chosen life in recovery over death in active addiction—effectively amputating that part of himself or herself engaged in the addiction—knows just how painful this choice can be.

A CLEAR CHOICE

In the portion of Hebrew Scripture known to Christians as the book of Deuteronomy, God—speaking through Moses—lays down a very clear choice: life or death, prosperity or adversity, blessings or curses. The Big Book of Alcoholics Anonymous poses a more fundamental proposition: "either God is everything or else He is nothing. God either is, or He isn't."[1] There is no middle ground, no grey area where we might fudge any of it. It's one or the other, and it's our choice.

Freedom of choice is one of God's most precious gifts to us, given from the very beginning, in the Garden of Eden. God created us, male and female, in his own image; he placed us in a world surrounded by abundance; he gave us dominion over all of it, with only one restriction; and he gave us total freedom of choice. Ever since that moment, we have been using, abusing, and struggling to understand this precious freedom.

BOUNDLESS FREEDOM, BOUNDED CHOICES

One of the things that we find so difficult to understand is that, whereas our *freedom* to choose is unlimited, our *choices* are not without boundaries. We are not the Creator; we are part of the created. As part of the created, we are not free to redefine Creation, to remake the world in our own image. Those of us who have attempted it can attest to the futility of the exercise. Reality is ours to discover, not ours to create.

> *Reality is ours to discover,*
>
> *not ours to create.*

A skydiver jumping out of an airplane at ten thousand feet can announce to the rest of her group: "I'm not using a parachute this time; I want total freedom!" She has total freedom to make that choice. Her choice, however, is subject to a higher law, in this case the law of gravity—a natural law of God's creation. If she chooses to accept the constraint of a parachute, she can enjoy her freedom within the larger context of the law. It is within that larger context that she will experience the consequences of her choices.

She has the fundamental freedom to choose, even if her choice is ultimately between life and death. So it is with us. God will never interfere in our freedom of choice—no matter how destructive our choices—because to do so would be to take back his own gift. He will never do that. As he has done since the beginning of time, however, God will always define the context within which we have total freedom.

For me, active addiction was not so much like a parachute jump from an airplane; it was more like a leap from the top of a tall building. At the beginning of my descent, for the first few floors, it was a real rush. It was fun, exhilarating, daring. Most of the trip, however, was pretty routine. The excitement was mostly gone. I ticked off floor after floor, always moving in the same general direction. It was only toward the end that it became truly terrifying, when I could see the ground coming up fast and realized that there was a sudden stop at the end of that free fall, a natural consequence of my free choice. I was going to die from choices that I had made in total freedom, unless I used that same freedom to make other choices.

Child psychologists discovered an interesting truth some years ago. Contemporary thought assumed that fences around playgrounds made the children feel restricted in their recreation. A consensus was reached to remove the fences, so the children wouldn't feel confined. But researchers discovered that just the opposite occurred. In the absence of fences, children became more inhibited with their activities. They tended to huddle toward the middle of the playground and exhibited signs of insecurity. Once the fences were replaced, the children played with greater enthusiasm and freedom.[2] All of us need boundaries, something to define the limits of safety and security. Boundaries may seem at first to restrict our

All of us need boundaries, something to define the limits of safety and security.

creativity; however, as the children on the playground demonstrated, we need a clear understanding of what is safe and acceptable, so that our creativity can flourish.

Just Say Yes

You may be familiar with the slogan: "Just Say No" to drugs. It was coined by First Lady Nancy Reagan during the summer of 1984 and became the banner for our nation's war on drugs. As effective as the slogan may be, it presents only half of the story. We understand that we cannot recover from active addiction unless we abstain from using drugs and alcohol. But the life that God has promised us, the life that is ours in recovery, is not just about saying no. It is mostly about saying yes. It is not so much freedom *from* as it is freedom *for*. It is about choosing life. It is the same choice that God gave to Adam and Eve. It is the same choice that God gave to the Hebrew nation three thousand years ago. And it is the choice that God gives to each of us. The focus is not the restricted freedom imposed by the boundaries, but rather the exhilarating freedom that is ours if we choose to live within the boundaries.

The focus is not the restricted freedom imposed by the boundaries, but rather the exhilarating freedom that is ours if we choose to live within the boundaries.

God's Chosen

I can identify with the ancient Israelites. They were a loose band of tribes that spent many years wandering in search of a home. I, too, wandered for many years, searching for someplace that felt like home. Eventually they settled in Egypt, which seemed to be a secure place. Under a new Egyptian pharaoh, however, they were enslaved and forced to live in bondage. I started out living in a secure place but then spent over half of my life in slavery to my addiction. Early on, God made a promise to Abraham that Israel would be a great nation, his chosen people. You and I are also among God's chosen people, living out of that same promise. God promised the Israelites after their years of suffering that they would be delivered from bondage, and God parted the Red Sea and led them to the Promised Land. It was through no less a miracle that God led me to the promised land of my recovery.

God's Covenant

Wherever the people of Israel went, God was very clear about the Law according to which they were to live. When they broke it, God spelled it out again; that's what we read in Deuteronomy, which means "second law," that is, a repetition of the first statement of the Law recorded in the book of Exodus. In the words from Deuteronomy, it is as clear and as immediate to us today as it was to the Israelites 3,500 years ago:

> If you obey the commandments of the LORD your God that I am commanding you today, by loving the LORD your God,

walking in his ways, and observing his commandments, decrees, and ordinances, then you shall live and become numerous, and the LORD your God will bless you in the land that you are entering to possess. But if your heart turns away and you do not hear, but are led astray to bow down to other gods and serve them, I declare to you today that you shall perish; you shall not live long in the land that you are crossing the Jordan to enter and possess. (Deut 30:16-18)

How much simpler can it be?

The psalm at the beginning of this chapter serves as a preface to the book of Psalms, the hymnbook of the Hebrew nation: "Happy are those . . . [whose] delight is in the law of the LORD. . . . They are like trees planted by streams of water, which yield their fruit in its season, and their leaves do not wither. In all that they do, they prosper" (Ps 1:1-3). It's the same message, and it's as clear and simple today as it has ever been.

NEW FREEDOM AND HAPPINESS

Following the description of the Ninth Step in the Big Book are the Twelve Promises, which some 12-Step groups read at every meeting. The first two Promises assure us that if we are "painstaking" about our recovery, "we are going to know a new freedom and a new happiness."[3] The freedom may be new to *us*, but it is not new to God. It is the very freedom that he gave us at Creation. It is freedom that we can reclaim, if we will choose to live according to the clear instructions that he has provided. In typically distilled clarity, the Big Book uses different words to say the same thing in the chapter entitled "How It Works":

This is the how and why of it. First of all, we had to quit playing God. It didn't work. Next, we decided that hereafter in this drama of life, God was going to be our Director. He is the Principal; we are His agents. He is the Father, and we are His children. Most good ideas are simple, and this concept was the keystone of the new and triumphant arch through which we passed to freedom.[4]

We can choose to remain bound by self-power or to be liberated by "a Power greater than ourselves [that can] restore us to sanity." We have total freedom to make that choice.

NEW BLESSEDNESS

The Big Book's promise of happiness relates directly to Scripture. Modern translations of the Bible often render the more traditional word *blessed* as *happy*; for example, the First Psalm begins "Blessed is the man" in the King James Version, but "Happy are those" in the New Revised Standard Version quoted above. Thus in coming to know a new *happiness*, as promised in the Big Book, we will actually come to know a new *blessedness*, as

> *The life we live is the one we wish to live. . . .*

promised in the Big Big Book (that is, the Bible). It really is a choice between blessings and curses, prosperity and adversity, life and death.

The twentieth-century religious writer Charles Allen tells the story of a wise man who always gave right answers to the difficult questions of life. One day an arrogant young man sought to trick the older sage by concealing a live bird in his hands and asking: "Sir, is the bird in my hands alive or dead?" His plan of deception was simple. If the wise senior said it was dead, then he would open his hands and let the bird fly away. If the man said it was alive, he would give his hands a quick squeeze and open them to reveal a dead bird. Surprisingly, the older man never looked at the younger man's hands. He looked deeply into his eyes and quietly said: "My son, it is whatever you wish it to be." Dr. Allen then wrote: "So it is with each of us. The life we live is the one we wish to live—God's way, or some other way. The choice is in our own hands."[5]

In coming to know a new happiness, *as promised in the Big Book, we will actually come to know a new* blessedness, *as promised in the Big Big Book.*

This is captured poignantly in a poem entitled "What's the Problem?" by Victor Fried:

What's the problem, said the old man,
    with concern in his eyes?
Can you tell me why you're sitting here,
    why don't you even try?
Can you tell me why you've let your heart
    become an empty well?
And I looked around my alley,
    and I told him, life is hell.

Then he smiled so soft and gentle,
   and he put his hand on mine,
and he said life is what you make it, son,
   and I think life is fine.
You see the world is filled with more good things
   than your mind can conceive,
but your heart is filled with just one thing,
   and that's whatever you believe.
Well, his words made me uncomfortable,
   they made me want to go,
yet, I sat and listened
   for reasons I don't know.
Perhaps it was his manner,
   perhaps it was his voice,
but I felt compelled to listen
   as if I had no choice.
He said if you believe your life is hell,
   then hell your life will be.
If you believe your life is beautiful,
   then your heart will be free.
If you believe life gives you nothing,
   then it's nothing you'll receive.
You see, you don't get what you want from life,
   you get what you believe.
Then suddenly, like magic,
   my life flashed before my eyes,
and I saw the things that I believed
   throughout my downhill slide.
When I believed I was a failure,
   then failure followed me,
and I heard my voice from somewhere say,
   help me change what I believe.
So, for many days thereafter,

we sat and talked alone,
    in that dark and dingy alleyway
        that had become my home.
Not a penny from his pocket
        did he ever offer me,
but he shared the secrets of his heart,
        and set my spirit free.
Well, many years have come and gone,
        since we first talked alone,
and I try hard to keep my feet
        upon the path he's shown.
Nothing in the world has changed,
        but something's changed in me.
Now I go back to those alleys
        looking for another me.
And what's the problem, I say to him,
        with concern in my eyes?
Can you tell me why you're sitting here,
        why don't you even try?
Can you tell me why you've let your heart
        become an empty well?
And he looks around at his alley,
        and he tells me, life is hell.
So, I pass on the wisdom
        that was once passed on to me,
that you need only change your mind
        for your heart to be free.
You see the world is filled with more good things
        than your mind can conceive,
but your heart is filled with just one thing,
        and that's whatever you believe.

WE LIVE IN THE PROMISED LAND

Every one of us in recovery lives in the promised land. We may have wandered for many years in the wilderness, but we have finally reached the land promised to us by God. It is a land of new freedom and new happiness, "a land flowing with milk and honey" (Exod 3:8), rather than booze and drugs; and it is by nothing less than a miracle that we have been brought here. God sets before us today the same choice that was set before the Israelites three thousand years ago: life or death, prosperity or adversity, blessings or curses. The choice is mine. The choice is yours. Choose life.

FOUR

BEGINNING AGAIN

*S*o when they had come together, they asked him, "Lord, is
this the time when you will restore the kingdom to Israel?"
He replied, "It is not for you to know the times or periods that
the Father has set by his own authority. But you will receive
power when the Holy Spirit has come upon you; and you will be
my witnesses in Jerusalem, in all Judea and Samaria, and to the
ends of the earth." When he had said this, as they were watching, he was lifted up, and a cloud took him out of their sight.
While he was going and they were gazing up toward heaven, suddenly two men in white robes stood by them. They said, "Men
of Galilee, why do you stand looking up toward heaven? This
Jesus, who has been taken up from you into heaven, will come
in the same way as you saw him go into heaven."

—Acts 1:6-11

Once we have chosen life over death, what then? After everything we've been through, how can we possibly start over?

———

Few recovering alcoholics or addicts—even those with decades
of sobriety—will ever forget their bottom, that life-changing

place of impenetrable darkness and gut-wrenching despair where we finally realize that we have nowhere to turn, and we don't see any point in trying. The Big Book describes some of the feelings commonly experienced in that place: loneliness, despair, self-pity, resentment, lethargy, bitterness, anger, nervousness, worry, helplessness, fear, weakness, misery, uselessness, guilt, unhappiness, bewilderment, shame—the list seems endless. When we finally reach that point where our life is falling apart faster than we can lower our standards, and we can finally muster the honesty to admit that we are powerless over this disease, and our life has become unmanageable by us, and we are willing to allow that there might be a better way, what do we do then?

Few recovering alcoholics or addicts—even those with decades of sobriety—will ever forget their bottom. . . .

The disciples who were present at the Ascension of Jesus, described above in the passage from the book of Acts, faced the same question as they watched their Lord leave them behind with only a vague promise that one day he would return. Some of them had been with Jesus throughout the three years of his public ministry. They had experienced a growing awareness that this man in their midst was indeed their long-awaited Messiah, the Son of God, King of the Jews, Redeemer of the world. Some expected that he would become a mighty warrior, rising up to vanquish the occupying Roman oppressors, freeing the Jews to be God's chosen people, "[restoring] the kingdom to Israel." Less than two months earlier, he had entered Jerusalem to loud cries of "Hosanna! Blessed is the one who comes in the name of the Lord!" (Mark 11:9). The Israelites seemed to be on the verge of liberation. Then came the trial, crucifixion, and burial. Just when they thought all was lost, he rose from the dead and appeared to some of them. Then he was gone, and they were left behind, confused and afraid, wondering what had become of him, and what would become of them. Had the entire Jesus event been nothing more than a dream, a hopeful fantasy of a desperate people who had known far too much slavery and oppression throughout their history? For those present that day, it must have felt like hitting bottom.

Like the disciples, after all that's happened, how do we begin again?

GOD CAN REPAIR OUR BROKEN LIFE

Victor Fried, the author of the poem "What's the Problem?" from chapter 3, recalls the point at which he began again. In his own words:

> For most of my life, I believed in God, but I hated him. Just as I believed in the police force, I knew it existed, but I didn't want to have anything to do with it. I had convinced myself that all my problems ultimately boiled down to one cause: God messing with me. Not only did I hate God, but I believed God hated me. And when you believe something strongly enough, your mind searches for evidence to support your belief and rejects all evidence to the contrary.

I was working part-time in a custom furniture shop. I had been sober for about a year and a half. I had turned my drinking over to God, but only my drinking; I wanted him to stay out of the rest of my life. Working in the furniture shop didn't pay much, so I was always looking for ways to make more money. One day, I was driving down the street, and I saw a man carrying an antique chair toward a dumpster. The chair had a broken rung, which I knew I could repair; then I could refinish the chair and make some money selling it.

I pulled up beside the dumpster and said to the man, "If you're going to throw that away, can I have it?"

"No," he snarled and smashed it over the side of the dumpster.

To me this was clearly evidence that God hated me, because he had offered me a chance to make some money and then jerked it away as soon as I reached for it.

One year later, I had reached a point where life was no longer worth living. I just didn't want to fight anymore. It was winter in Kansas City during a bad cold snap with subzero temperatures. I drove my car along the Missouri River, parked, and walked a long way downstream. I was wearing a heavy coat that I thought would help the current pull me under—knowing that I was a coward and, as soon as I hit that icy water, I would probably try to get to the shore. I walked far enough from my car to ensure that, if I did somehow make it out of the water alive, I would surely freeze to death before I could get back to it.

While standing on the river bank, taking one last look around, watching chunks of ice float down the river, suddenly instead of chunks of ice, I saw that dumpster, and I saw that antique chair; and I heard a voice right behind me, and the voice said, "If you're going to throw that away, can I have it?"

Many people would say that was a hallucination brought on by deep depression, and they can believe that if they wish; but I knew it was the voice of God. The same God that I had spent my life hating had not hated me back. As I looked at that river, I suddenly saw the face of every human being I had ever hurt throughout my life—and there were a lot of them—from people whose feelings I had hurt to people I had put in the Emergency Room with my bare hands. And I realized that, despite all of that, God still loved me—not because of who *I* am, but because of who *he* is. And I decided that, if he could fix me and use me, he could have me. I had no idea at the time what that meant. I just knew that I didn't want to run the show anymore.[1]

God has a plan for all of us, just as he had for the disciples who watched Jesus depart. As with the disciples, the decision to participate in God's plan is totally ours to make.

Jesus understood the disappointment that his disciples felt as he left them. In his parting words, he called them to a new mission of witness empowered by the Holy Spirit. He called them to begin again.

THE NEED TO BEGIN AGAIN

The need to begin again is not new. The call goes back almost to the beginning of Creation, when Adam and Eve disobeyed God's instructions and were driven out from the Garden of Eden. Had they not had the courage to begin again, that would have been the end of humankind. But they did begin again, and so must we.

One of the Big Book's Twelve Promises, which were mentioned in chapter 3, is: "We will not regret the past nor wish to shut the door on it."[2] That's what the disciples did after the Ascension. They did not regret their years with Jesus. On the contrary, energized by their Higher Power, they used the experiences from their former life to enrich their new life, as they spread the message of the Gospel throughout the civilized world. We can do that, as well. Energized by *our* Higher Power, we can use the experiences of *our* former life to enrich *our* new life, as we carry the message of recovery to all who need to hear it.

> *The decision to participate in God's plan is totally ours to make.*

Holocaust survivor and Nobel Peace Prize–winner Elie Wiesel understands the importance of beginning again. He wrote: "When God created us, God gave Adam a secret—and that secret was not how to begin, but how to begin again. In other words, it is not given to us to begin; that privilege is God's alone. But it is given to us to begin again—and we do every time we choose to defy death and side with the living."[3] Every one of us in recovery has made that choice: "to defy death and side with the living."

> *When God created us, God gave Adam a secret—and that secret was not how to begin, but how to begin again.*
> *—Elie Wiesel*

How Can We Begin Again?

There is one absolute requirement for beginning again: We must be willing to let go of the past. We have a saying in AA: "Yesterday is history, tomorrow is a mystery, today is a gift." That's why we call it the "present." Unless we can deal responsibly with what the Big Book calls "the wreckage of our past," make appropriate amends, and then let it go, we will never be able to live fully in the present, and we will have no future in recovery. We must make peace with yesterday if we are to have the today and the tomorrow that our Higher Power intends for us. And one of the most important things to understand about the past is: no matter what has happened, it has all worked together to bring us to this very moment; and this is the moment when we can choose to make everything new, to begin again.

There is a beautiful little poem attributed to Kathleen Wheeler and entitled "A New Leaf" that captures God's gift of beginning again:

> He came to my desk with a quivering lip; the lesson was done.
> "Have you a new sheet for me, dear teacher? I've spoiled this one."
> I took his sheet, all soiled and blotted, and gave him a new one all unspotted.
> And into his tired heart I cried, "Do better now, my child."
> I went to the throne with a trembling heart; the day was done.
> "Have you a new day for me, dear Master? I've spoiled this one."
> He took my day, all soiled and blotted and gave me a new one all unspotted.
> And into my tired heart he cried, "Do better now, my child."

Every one of us in recovery can receive a new leaf every day, as we turn our will and our life over to the care of God as we understand God, and accept from God's loving hand the blessed gift of a new day "all unspotted," to live in only for that one day.

There is a true story of a priest who was much loved, but who carried a secret burden of a long-past sin deep in his heart. He had committed that sin during his time in seminary. No one else knew about it. He had repented of it and suffered remorse for it but had never felt the peace of God's forgiveness.

A woman in his parish who claimed to have visions in which she spoke with Christ, came to visit this priest. The priest was skeptical of her claims, so to test her visions, he said to her: "You say you actually speak directly to the Lord in your visions. Let me ask you a favor. The next time you have one of those visions, I want you to ask him what sin your priest committed while he was in seminary." The woman agreed and went back home.

God forgives without exceptions.

When she returned a few days later, the priest said: "Well, did Christ visit you in your dreams?"

"Yes, he did," she replied.

"And did you ask him what sin I committed in seminary?"

"Yes, I asked him."

"Well, what did he say?"

The woman paused, and then replied: "He said, 'I don't remember.' "

The psalmist wrote: "Happy are those whose transgression is forgiven, whose sin is covered" (Ps 32:1). Or as one pastor expressed it: "Bury your sins in the deepest part of the ocean, and God will hang a sign there that says: 'No Fishing.'" God bears no grudges, and God forgives without exceptions. It is we who insist on carrying with us our past sins with all of their oppressive weight, until we finally learn to let go.

LETTING GO OF THE PAST

The key to letting go of our past is forgiveness. Regardless of the mistakes you have made, a loving, merciful God has written across every page of your life's story one word: "Forgiven." Some of the best news comes to us from God through the book of Isaiah:

- "Do not fear, for I have redeemed you" (43:1b).
- "Do not remember the former things, or consider the things of old" (43:18).
- "I, I am He who blots out your transgressions for my own sake, and I will not remember your sins" (43:25).
- "I have swept away your transgressions like a cloud, and your sins like mist; return to me, for I have redeemed you" (44:22).

God's forgiveness is not like a health insurance policy with exemptions for pre-existing conditions. With God, there are no pre-existing conditions. God's forgiveness is absolute, total, eternal. We have only to accept it. God can forgive anything, if we repent; and God has always had more use for the broken and repentant than for the high and mighty.

Many years ago, there was a distinguished minister in Boston who was continually harassed by a woman in his congregation. She started vicious rumors about him. She circulated petitions to have him fired. Although he tried everything he knew to resolve the problem, she would accept no offer of reconciliation. Finally, her husband was transferred to another city, so they moved away.

The key to letting go of our past is forgiveness.

Soon thereafter she was profoundly converted and became a genuine Christian. In the days that followed, her conscience was haunted by the memories of how she had treated her former pastor. So she sat down and wrote him a long letter, telling what had happened in her life, and begging him to forgive the awful way she had treated him. In reply, she received a telegram from the pastor. When she read it, she wept with joy. It contained just three words: FORGIVEN, FORGOTTEN, FOREVER! You and I have received that same telegram. It has our name on it. It was sent long-distance over two thousand years straight from a hill on the outskirts of Jerusalem with an empty cross on it, and that telegram still reads: FORGIVEN, FORGOTTEN, FOREVER!

THE LAND OF BEGINNING AGAIN

Louisa Fletcher understood both the family devastation caused by alcohol abuse and the necessity to begin again. Louisa was the daughter of a nationally prominent Indianapolis banker. In 1902, she married Pulitzer Prize–winning author Booth Tarkington, whose progressive abuse of alcohol led to the painful collapse of the marriage in just nine years. In 1911, the year of her divorce, Louisa Fletcher Tarkington published a poem entitled "The Land of Beginning Again":

Won't you travel with me on the highway of life?
Down the road of Forgive and Forget
That leads to the Land of Beginning Again
Where old friends are better friends yet.

I wish that there were some wonderful place
Called the Land of Beginning Again,
Where all our mistakes and all our heartaches
And all of our poor selfish grief
Could be dropped like a shabby old coat at the door
And never be put on again.

I wish we might come on it all unaware,
Like the hunter who finds a lost trail;
And I wish that the one whom our blindness had done
The greatest injustice of all,
Could be there at the gates like an old friend who waits
For the comrade he's gladdest to hail.

We would find all the things we intended to do
But forgot, and remembered too late:
Little praises unspoken, little promises broken,
And all the thousand and one
Little duties neglected that might have perfected
The day for one less fortunate.

It wouldn't be possible not to be kind
In the Land of Beginning Again,
And the ones we misjudged and the ones whom we grudged
Their moments of victory here
Would find in the grasp of our loving hand-clasp
More than penitent lip could explain.

For what had been hardest, we'd know had been best,
And what had seemed loss would be gain.
For there isn't a sting that will not take wing
When we've faced it and laughed it away.
And I think that the laughter is most what we're after
In the Land of Beginning Again.

So I wish that there were some wonderful place
Called the Land of Beginning Again,
Where all our mistakes and all our heartaches
And all of our poor selfish grief
Could be dropped like a shabby old coat at the door
And never be put on again.

There *is* a Land of Beginning Again for anyone suffering from addiction. It is the land of 12-Step recovery. Regardless of the

Everything has become new.

—2 Cor 5:17

depth of the pit where we finally hit bottom, those of us in recovery have a twelve-step ladder that we can climb, one step at a time. When we reach the twelfth step, we place another twelve-step section of that ladder on top of the last one, and we begin again on another first step. Energized by our Higher Power, we do that over and over, climbing one twelve-step section after another, until we emerge from the impenetrable darkness of that pit into the brilliant light of continuous sobriety. We begin again, embracing God's assurance to us: "See, I am making all things new" (Rev 21:5). The apostle Paul wrote to the Corinthians: "So if anyone is in Christ, there is a new creation: everything old has passed away; see, everything has become new!" (2 Cor 5:17).

We have no control over what has happened to us, but we have total control over what we do about what has happened to us.

We have no control over what has happened to us, but we have *total control* over what we do about what has happened to us. We can choose to cling to the old things that have "passed away," or we can choose to live in God's new creation, where "everything has become new." This is the Land of Beginning Again, "where all our mistakes and all our heartaches and all of our poor selfish grief [can] be dropped like a shabby old coat at the door and never be put on again."

So, as we, like the disciples, turn away from the life we have known toward the new life that awaits us, let us read again our telegram from Calvary: FORGIVEN, FORGOTTEN, FOR-EVER! Let us accept God's unconditional gift of forgiveness—absolute, total, eternal. And let us walk confidently, one step at a time, from the enveloping darkness of our old life into the glorious light of God's new creation, where we can be at last, in the words of our Big Book, "happy, joyous, and free."[4] Welcome to the Land of Beginning Again!

FIVE

GATHER UP THE
FRAGMENTS

*A*fter this Jesus went to the other side of the Sea of Galilee,
also called the Sea of Tiberias. A large crowd kept following him, because they saw the signs that he was doing for the
sick. Jesus went up the mountain and sat down there with his disciples. Now the Passover, the festival of the Jews, was near.
When he looked up and saw a large crowd coming toward him,
Jesus said to Philip, "Where are we to buy bread for these people
to eat?" He said this to test him, for he himself knew what he was
going to do. Philip answered him, "Six months' wages would not
buy enough bread for each of them to get a little." One of his disciples, Andrew, Simon Peter's brother, said to him, "There is a
boy here who has five barley loaves and two fish. But what are
they among so many people?" Jesus said, "Make the people sit
down." Now there was a great deal of grass in the place; so they
sat down, about five thousand in all. Then Jesus took the loaves,
and when he had given thanks, he distributed them to those who
were seated; so also the fish, as much as they wanted. When they
were satisfied, he told his disciples, "Gather up the fragments left
over, so that nothing may be lost." So they gathered them up, and
from the fragments of the five barley loaves, left by those who had
eaten, they filled twelve baskets. When the people saw the sign

that he had done, they began to say, "This is indeed the prophet who is to come into the world."

—John 6:1-14

Life in early recovery is often littered with the disastrous consequences of our active addiction. As we survey the pieces of our life that lie scattered around us, how do we put it all back together? How can our Higher Power help?

The story is very familiar to us, regardless of our faith tradition. It is the feeding of the five thousand, or the miracle of the loaves and fishes, the only miracle of Jesus recorded in all four Gospels (Matt 14:13-21; Mark 6:30-44; Luke 9:10b-17; John 6:1-14) and the inspiration for thousands of restaurants, coffee houses, and similar establishments worldwide whose names refer to "loaves and fishes."

The setting for the story is a desolate place on the northern shore of the Sea of Galilee. A great crowd had been following Jesus, who had been teaching and healing the sick throughout the day. His twelve disciples had been with him the whole time. It was hot, they were tired, and they had not eaten anything. According to the accounts in Matthew, Mark, and Luke, one of the disciples said to Jesus: "This is a deserted place, and the hour is very late; send the crowds away so that they may go into the villages and buy food for themselves." Jesus replied: "You give them something to eat." The disciples responded as any of us might well respond: "Who . . . us? With what? It would cost over six months' wages to buy enough bread to feed all these people. All we have are five loaves of bread and two fish." Jesus said: "Bring them here to me." And he took the five loaves and the two fish, looked up to heaven, blessed and broke the loaves, and gave them to the disciples.

These were the familiar actions of a host at a typical Jewish meal. The blessing was probably the traditional Jewish blessing: "Blessed are you, O Lord our God, king of the universe, who brings forth bread from the earth."

Jesus would later perform the same actions with different bread—taking, blessing, breaking, giving—at the Last Supper on the night he was handed over to death. These same four actions occur every time we celebrate the miracle of the Eucharist, or Holy Communion, by which Jesus' followers have been fed to the present day with spiritual food.

In the Galilean wilderness, the disciples distributed the pieces of bread and the fish to the crowd, which, we are told, numbered five thousand men. This would have been according to the ancient convention of counting families by the heads of households. Including women and children, the number of people was undoubtedly much higher. "And all ate and were filled." Afterward, Jesus told the disciples: "Gather up the fragments left over, so that nothing may be lost." The disciples gathered up the fragments that lay scattered around them, and the leftovers filled twelve of the large, heavy, wicker baskets that were commonly used by the poorer classes of Jews to carry food.

GOD FEEDS HIS WORLD

Beyond the popularity of the story, I believe there are several important insights that we can gain from this miracle. First, it is God's will that the hungry be fed. Images of this reality were very much part of the Hebrew tradition shared by the predominantly Jewish crowd assembled that day by the Sea of Galilee. Approximately 1,400 years earlier, while their ancestors had wandered in the desert seeking the Promised Land, God had fed them with manna (bread) from heaven (Exod 16:1-36; Num 11:4-9). Five hundred years after that, one of their greatest prophets, Elisha, had ordered his servant to set twenty loaves of barley and some fresh ears of corn before a hundred men; and everyone was fed, with some left over (2 Kgs 4:42-44). God was about to perform a similar miracle in another wilderness through another prophet. Once again, all would eat until they were full, and there would be food left over.

It is God's will that the hungry be fed.

In our Eleventh Step, we pray for knowledge of God's will for us and the power to carry out his will. If it is God's will that hungry people are fed, how does that involve us?

GOD NEEDS OUR HELP

The second insight I believe we can derive from this miracle answers that question: God needs each one of us to assist in the feeding of this world. This is not just about food. The Hebrew

Wisdom Literature often equates teaching with feeding and learning wisdom with eating bread. Jesus fed the crowd first with the spiritual food of his teaching and then with the physical food of the loaves and fishes. This is what we do in the program of Alcoholics Anonymous when we feed each other with the spiritual food of our "experience, strength, and hope." It is the basis for all of our service

God is calling each of us to help feed this hungry world.

work. It took me almost fifty years to realize that I was not put on this earth to be a blessing to myself. I was put here to be a blessing to others. My life has meaning only in the ways in which I use the gifts God has given me to help others. We feed each other by sharing what we have been given.

The epilogue to the Gospel of John describes an appearance of Jesus to the disciples following his resurrection. On the shore of this same lake, he asked Simon Peter three times: "Do you love me?" Three times Peter assured Jesus that Peter loved him. Jesus responded: "Feed my sheep" (John 21:15-17). Jesus speaks those same words to each of us today. The disciples in our story wanted to send the crowd away to find their own food. How many people do *we* send away to find their own nourishment, when all the while God is calling each of us to help feed this hungry world?

GOD USES OUR GIFTS

A third lesson we can learn from this miracle is that our gifts—however insignificant they may seem—when placed in God's hands are sufficient to accomplish God's purpose. When Jesus told the disciples that they should feed the crowd, they reacted understandably: "How can we possibly feed this many people with only five loaves of bread and two fish?" And they were right. There is no way through human devices to feed so many people with so little food; but God can.

Our gifts . . . when placed in God's hands are sufficient to accomplish God's purpose.

The disciples made the same mistake we make over and over again. We live in the illusion that we are solely responsible for our accomplishments, which may be why we accomplish so little. In our self-centered ego—which the Big Book tells us is "the root of our troubles"—we are in control, and God is an afterthought. In reality, we are powerless and can do nothing without God, who strengthens us. There are no theatrics in the feeding miracle. Jesus did not take the loaves and fishes, hold them up for all to see, mutter some magic words, and create a mountain of bread and fish to be distributed to the crowd. He took what little he had, blessed it, broke it, and gave it to his disciples; and they began to distribute pieces of only five loaves and two fishes. They didn't stop to complain that this was enough for only a few people. They gave, and gave, and gave some more, and there was more than enough. It was in the giving that the miracle happened.

There are two other messages buried in the details of this story that only John's Gospel tells us. First, the source of the bread and fish was a young boy—not a wealthy, powerful man with vast resources to share, but one of the powerless of that society. How often do we feel that we just aren't strong enough, smart enough, good enough to be of use to God? And yet, in this story, it was a young boy from whose meager offering the miracle grew in Jesus' hands. In God's sight, not one of us, with our unique way of being and responding, is ever overlooked in the crowds.

The second detail recorded only in John's account is that the bread was made from barley. Barley bread was cheap, only a third the cost of wheat bread. It was bread eaten by the poor. It was this bread, made from the most common of grains, that Jesus used to feed all who were hungry, and there were large baskets full of leftovers. So it is with our gifts. In our hands, they may seem small, common. In God's hands, they can feed a multitude.

What gifts can you bring to God for his next miracle?

GATHERING UP THE FRAGMENTS

Perhaps the most powerful lesson for those of us in recovery comes at the end of the story. All have eaten until they are satisfied. The banquet is finished. And Jesus tells the disciples to "gather up the fragments left over, so that nothing may be lost." In my active addiction, I approached life as if it were a banquet of a different sort. Everything was there for me to use, to consume; and my addiction ate everything in sight, including most of me. When the banquet was finally over, there were only fragments left. My life today is a result of the gathering up of those fragments.

One of my favorite stories in recovery concerns another young boy. He was in the second grade, and his year-end class project was to make a gift for one of his parents. He knew how much his father enjoyed smoking his pipe. He would make a special ashtray. It would be the perfect gift for his dad. He worked hard to shape the clay just right. After it had been fired, he painted it bright blue, his father's favorite color. He was so excited that he could hardly wait for the end of the school year. When it finally came, parents and teachers and students gathered for one last open house. After the program, the little boy rushed to his locker to retrieve his treasure. The moment was here at last. As he ran down the hall toward his parents, he tripped and fell. The ashtray hit the floor and shattered across the hallway. Weeks of loving work and eager anticipation lay in pieces around him. All he could do was sit and cry. His father, a retired military officer, came over to him and said: "It's all right, Son. It's not that important. Stop crying now. Be a man." But his mother stooped down, gently put her arm around his shoulders, and said: "I'm so sorry, honey. I know how important this is. Let me help you gather up the pieces, and we'll see what we can make from them."

When we place our brokenness into God's hands, we will be healed, restored to wholeness, transformed into abundant life.

Like that little boy, when I first got into recovery, I sat where I had finally hit bottom. My life, once a cherished treasure full of promise, lay scattered in pieces all around me—dreams broken, hopes shattered—and all I could do was weep. And God stooped down beside me, gently put his arm around my shoulders, and said: "I'm so sorry. I know how important this is. Let me help you gather up the pieces, and we'll see what we can make from them." My life today in recovery, overflowing with love and joy and hope, is what God and I have been able to make from those pieces.

The future for every one of us is based not on what we've lost, but rather on what we have left. Even if all we bring are the shattered pieces of our life, when we place our brokenness into God's hands, we will be healed, restored to wholeness, transformed into abundant life.

It is God's will that all should be fed, and God needs our help. We are the modern-day disciples who distribute the gifts that God so miraculously multiplies in our hands. And just as Jesus did by the Sea of Galilee so long ago, we must continue to feed each other, in the blessed assurance that, if

> *The future for every one of us is based not on what we've lost, but rather on what we have left.*

we but place our gifts into God's hands—no matter how meager those gifts may seem to us—God will multiply our simple "barley loaves" many times over; and through this miracle we will be able to feed all who come to us for spiritual nourishment, assistance, and encouragement. And all will be filled, and nothing—not a single fragment—will be lost.

SIX

YOU ARE CALLED
BY NAME

I *waited patiently for the* LORD;
   he inclined to me and heard my cry.
He drew me up from the desolate pit,
   out of the miry bog,
and set my feet upon a rock,
   making my steps secure.
He put a new song in my mouth,
   a song of praise to our God.
Many will see and fear,
   and put their trust in the LORD.

Happy are those who make
   the Lord their trust,
who do not turn to the proud,
   to those who go astray after false gods. . . .

Do not, O LORD, *withhold*
   your mercy from me;
let your steadfast love and your faithfulness
   keep me safe forever. . . .

61

Be pleased, O LORD, to deliver me;
   O LORD, make haste to help me. . . .
You are my help and my deliverer;
   do not delay, O my God.

—Psalm 40:1-4, 11, 13, 17b

But now thus says the LORD, he who created you, O Jacob,
   he who formed you, O Israel:
Do not fear, for I have redeemed you;
   I have called you by name, you are mine.
When you pass through the waters, I will be with you;
   and through the rivers, they shall not overwhelm you;
when you walk through fire you shall not be burned,
   and the flame shall not consume you.
For I am the LORD your God,
   the Holy One of Israel, your Savior. . . .

Bring forth the people who are blind, yet have eyes,
   who are deaf, yet have ears! . . .

I, I am the LORD,
   and besides me there is no savior. . . .

I, I am He
   who blots out your transgressions for my own sake,
   and I will not remember your sins. . . .

I will give you the treasures of darkness
   and riches hidden in secret places,

so that you may know that it is I, the LORD,
  the God of Israel, who call you by your name.
For the sake of my servant Jacob,
  and Israel my chosen,
I call you by your name,
  I surname you, though you do not know me. . . .

Turn to me and be saved,
  all the ends of the earth!
For I am God, and there is no other.
                              —Isaiah 43:1-3a, 8, 11, 25; 45:3, 4, 22

We who have made it into recovery are all too familiar with the psalmist's "desolate pit" or "miry bog," that place of abject despair out of which God calls us. That God calls each of us *by name* is nothing less than a personal invitation into a personal relationship with our Higher Power, the God of our understanding.

———— ———— ————

"What's in a name?" mused Shakespeare's Juliet. "That which we call a rose by any other name would smell as sweet." As the familiar story unfolds, however, Juliet's youthful naïveté is soon swept away by tragic reality, as she and her beloved Romeo die ultimately because of the power of a name.

Naming has been important since the beginning of time, from the earliest account of Creation in the book of Genesis, in which Adam "gave names to all cattle, and to the birds of the air, and to every animal of the field . . . ." (see Gen 2:18-20a).

In ancient thought, to name something was to have power over it. Adam's naming of all the creatures of the earth was God's way of giving humankind dominion over Creation. Even today, Orthodox Jews neither pronounce nor write completely the name of God, because to name God would imply having power over the deity. In ancient times, a name was not a mere label of identification; it was an expression of the essential nature of the being. Hence to know the *name* of God was to know the *nature* of God, as God revealed himself.

Throughout the Bible, names are given great importance; in fact, various forms of the word *name* appear in the Bible no fewer than 1,136 times. A name captured the essence of a personality, an expression of innermost being. When God called Abraham, he did it with these words: "I will make of you a great nation, and I will bless you, and make your name great, so that you will be a blessing. I will bless those who bless you, and the one who curses you I will curse; and in you all the families of the earth shall be blessed" (Gen 12:2, 3). Abraham's original name, Abram, meant "exalted ancestor." The meaning of the name was so important that God changed Abraham's name to fit his new role, as "ancestor of a multitude."

Scripture contains many other examples illustrating the importance of naming, including the naming of Jesus. You may remember the scene from Matthew's Gospel, where Joseph has just learned that Mary, his fiancée, is pregnant and has resolved to divorce her quietly. "But just when he had resolved to do this, an angel of the Lord appeared to him in a dream and said, 'Joseph, son of David, do not be afraid to take Mary as your wife, for the child conceived in her is from the Holy Spirit. She will bear a son, and you are to name him Jesus [the Greek form of the Hebrew name *Joshua*, which meant "Deliverer" or "Savior"], for he will save his people from their sins.' All this took place to fulfill what had been spoken by the Lord through the prophet: 'Look, the virgin shall conceive and bear a son, and they shall name him Emmanuel,' which means, 'God is with us' " (Matt 1:20-23). Later he was called the Christ, which meant "anointed one." Names are important.

WHAT'S IN A NAME?

How important is your name? How do you feel when someone calls you by name? You may remember the television sitcom *Cheers*, in which there was a recurring scene whenever George Wendt's character entered the bar, and everyone shouted: "Norm!" The importance of the scene was captured in the theme song, which proclaimed: "You want to go where everybody knows your name." There is comfort in being in a place where everybody knows our name.

God knows our name. From the depths of wherever we are, God calls us by name. As an alcoholic saved from active addiction, the words of the Scripture passage opening the chapter resonate with me: "Bring forth the people who are blind, yet have eyes, who are deaf, yet have ears!" (Isa 43:8); and so do the words of our psalm: "He drew me up from the desolate pit, out of the miry bog, and set my feet upon a rock, making my steps secure" (Ps 40:2). In my active addition, I was blind, yet I had eyes; I was deaf, yet I had ears; and my life was a desolate pit, a miry bog sucking me constantly downward toward certain death.

From the depths of such darkness, God speaks to us through the words of the prophet: "Do not fear, for I have redeemed you; I have called you by name, you are mine" (Isa 43:1b). From the depths of that pit, he called me by name. In my recovery, he "set my feet upon a rock, making my steps secure" (Ps 40:2).

But why would God want me, a miserable alcoholic who had done so many shameful things? Why would he call me? The answer is very simple: God's love for me has absolutely nothing to do with what I have done, or what I have, or what I know, or what I look like, or what others think of me. God loves me simply because I am his child. In calling me by name, God claims not the person I think I am or the person others may think I am; God claims me as the person I am in God's sight.

God's love for me has absolutely nothing to do with what I have done, or what I have, or what I know, or what I look like, or what others think of me.

Too often we see ourselves as defined by our past or present circumstances, but God knows who we really are. Jesus said that every hair on our head is counted by God (Matt 10:30). From the moment of our creation, long before our birth, before we or anyone else could judge us, God knew us and loved us. As God said to the prophet Jeremiah so long ago: "Before I formed you in the womb I knew you, and before you were born I consecrated you" (Jer 1:5a). Just as the shepherd "calls his own sheep by name" (John 10:3b), God calls each of us by name. In calling us by name, God reaches out to the essence of our true self.

What does God hope to find in our essence? In her marvelous book that I described in the preface, *A Tree Full of Angels*, the Benedictine sister Macrina Wiederkehr writes:

> What God most longs to discover in us is our willingness to embrace ourselves as we are at our beginning—empty, little, and poor. Our willingness gives God free space within us to work out the Divine Plan. Our potential for greatness is tremendous. Acceptance of our littleness makes it possible for our greatness to emerge. Our littleness is not a choice. It is simply the way we are. Our greatness, however, is a choice. When we choose to accept the life God has given to us, when we allow God to fill our emptiness, we are choosing greatness.[1]

In a poem expressing this, she concludes:

> And then from within me, your voice came
> giving me a name that was new
> Little-Great-One, you called out, Come closer
> Little-Great-One, Beloved, Come home
> Come home to the self I keep loving
> Come home to the truth that you are
> Little-Great-One, you called out, Come closer
> Little-Great-One, you kept saying, Come home.
> You came with your all to my nothing
> With such reverence you called out my name

> You lifted me back into my poverty
> the littleness I was trying to escape
> Embracing that poverty, I felt wealthy
> I was free at last to be great.[2]

It is this return to the utter powerlessness of our core essence that is required in the First Step of our Program, and it is out of this powerlessness that we turn to our Higher Power for help.

Years ago in midtown Manhattan there was a young boy who sold newspapers on 50th Street, between Saks Fifth Avenue and Saint Patrick's Cathedral. One of the priests of the cathedral noticed that, sometime during most days, the lad would come into the cathedral and enter one of the side chapels. Sometimes the priest could hear the boy talking, as he knelt at the altar rail.

One day, encountering the boy as he emerged from the chapel, the priest said to him: "Tell me, what do you talk about in there?"

"Well," said the boy, "I start by saying, 'Jesus, this is Timmy,' and then I just talk to him."

Late one afternoon, as the priest was leaving the cathedral, he saw a large crowd gathered at the side of the church. As he made his way through the people, he saw that there had been an accident. On his way across the street to the cathedral, the newspaper boy had been hit by a car rounding the corner. He lay there, badly injured. When the ambulance arrived, the priest identified himself and asked if he could ride with the boy in the ambulance. As they set out for the hospital through the streets of New York, siren screaming, the boy lay in the back of the ambulance, barely breathing. Suddenly he sat bolt upright, his eyes wide open. A broad smile spread over his little face. Then he closed his eyes, lay back, and stopped breathing. The priest later said that, at that moment, above the sounds of the motor, the siren, and all the traffic, he heard an unmistakable, clear voice, saying: "Timmy, this is Jesus." You and I can live every day in a first-name relationship with our Higher Power.

Our Father, who art in heaven, how do you know my name? The astounding reality is that God does know my name—and your name. God calls each of us by name. God calls us out of our desolate pit, out of our miry bog. God calls us to come home to the littleness of our beginning and the greatness of God's plan for us. God calls us by name. Come home.

SEVEN

CLAIMING OUR AUTHENTIC SELF

A s God's chosen ones, holy and beloved, clothe yourselves with compassion, kindness, humility, meekness, and patience. Bear with one another and, if anyone has a complaint against another, forgive each other; just as the Lord has forgiven you, so you also must forgive. Above all, clothe yourselves with love, which binds everything together in perfect harmony. And let the peace of Christ rule in your hearts, to which indeed you were called in the one body. And be thankful. Let the word of Christ dwell in you richly; teach and admonish one another in all wisdom; and with gratitude in your hearts sing psalms, hymns, and spiritual songs to God. And whatever you do, in word or deed, do everything in the name of the Lord Jesus, giving thanks to God the Father through him.

—Colossians 3:12-17

Beginning on the day of our birth, we all experience unmet needs. Psychologists tell us that we respond to unmet needs by constructing a "false self," a system of masks and other defense mechanisms designed to protect us from the pain caused by those unmet needs. We surround our vulnerable core with one protective barrier upon another, like the layers of an onion, until we can no longer reach our genuine center. Much of our work in recovery—indeed, all spiritual formation—involves peeling back the layers of our false self in a journey to our authentic core, our "true self," as we were made originally in the perfect image and likeness of God. It is out of that authenticity that we seek to live in recovery. What models do we have for such authentic living? What examples can we follow, as we take our "searching and fearless moral inventory of ourselves" and humbly ask God to remove our shortcomings?

—※— —※— —※—

Beginning in the 1990s, many Christians displayed on an article of clothing, a piece of jewelry, or a bumper sticker the abbreviation *WWJD* (What Would Jesus Do?). It was intended as a reminder to measure behavior against the moral example of Jesus. The abbreviation and concept first became popular in 1897 with a novel by Charles Sheldon entitled *In His Steps: What Would Jesus Do?* that has sold more than thirty million copies (roughly the circulation of the Big Book). The four-part devotional classic entitled *The Imitation of Christ*, a handbook for daily living attributed to the German monk Thomas à Kempis, since its publication in the 1400s has been circulated in more than two thousand editions and is still in print; only the Bible has been read by more people in more translations. Since the days of the early church nearly two thousand years ago, theologians have debated the nature of the *imago Dei*, the "image of God," in which we are said to have been created. Human beings have long sought an ideal image after which to pattern their lives.

In whose image do you live? Is it the image of a parent or grand-parent? Is it the image of a spouse or partner? Is it the image of a teacher or friend? Or is it the image of God? What do you believe about what God believes about you? How do you let what God believes about you become the understanding out of which you live, rather than the messages you have gotten from other people, or from yourself?

IN THE BEGINNING

The book of Genesis in the Bible contains two narratives of Creation. The older of the two, from around 1,000 B.C.E., is in the second chapter. The later narrative, in the first chapter of Genesis, was probably written some 450 years later. The two narratives are very different, but taken together they offer a composite describing God's creation of the universe. No matter the order of events or how much time it took, we understand that God created the environment, all the plants and animals, and humankind, male and female. With regard to the creation of humankind, the later account is very explicit: "Then God said, 'Let us make humankind in our image, according to our likeness. . . .' So God created humankind in his image, in the image of God he created them; male and female he created them" (Gen 1:26a, 27). You and I are direct descendants of those first human beings. Like them, we have God's DNA; we were created in the image of God. What does that mean to us? What does God expect of us as creations in God's image?

GOD'S EXPECTATIONS OF US

God's expectations of us have been clearly articulated for thousands of years. Just as the Big Book contains instructions for living a clean and sober life, so the Big Big Book contains instructions for living a godly life. We have ancient Hebrew law, summarized by God and delivered to Moses in the form of the Ten Commandments. We have interpretations of the Law by the prophets, like the summary attributed to the prophet we call Micah: "What does the LORD require of you but to do justice, and to love kindness, and to walk humbly with your God?" (Mic 6:8b). In the New Testament we have the Beatitudes and other teachings of Jesus. We have the Great Commandment: "You shall love the Lord your God with all your

In whose image do you live?

heart, and with all your soul, and with all your strength, and with all your mind; and your neighbor as yourself" (Luke 10:27). We have interpretations of the apostles and other leaders of the early church, such as the summary instructions to the Colossians quoted at the head of this chapter. The instructions are direct and clear. But it is not sufficient simply to read these things, or even to understand them thoroughly. We must internalize them. We must make them our own, if we are to live into the image in which God created us. Just as recovery is about transformation, rather than information, the instructions are useless unless they inform how we live.

NO OTHER GODS

"You shall have no other gods before me." This is the First Commandment in the Old Law and the cornerstone of the godly life. This one principle orders the rest of life. When you get right down to it, there are no atheists. Everyone has a god, something or someone we respect, serve, perhaps even worship, above all else. For some people it's success, for others money, material possessions, relationships, sex, alcohol, drugs, food. Whatever we place at the top is our god. We have total freedom over the choice, but whatever we choose will set up our whole value system, determine our priorities, influence our decisions, and order our lives.

That's why this is the First Commandment. If we keep this commandment, placing God at the head of our lives, then everything else falls into place. We will live into the image of God in which we were created. When we place anything other than God at the head of our lives, we are trying to make God in *our* image, and, as some of us have gone to great lengths to prove, the results of such a choice can be disastrous. The psalmist wrote: "But they [that] run after another [God], shall have great trouble" (Ps 16:4 Coverdale's Bible).[1] How much misery have we experienced trying to recreate the world according to our priorities, instead of coming home to the way it actually is, the way God created it?

How much misery have we experienced trying to recreate the world according to our priorities, instead of coming home to the way it actually is, the way God created it?

I begin every day the same way: I wake up with untreated alcoholism. How I treat it is my responsibility, and that reality determines, in many ways, how I live that day. But I wake up with another reality even more powerful: I was created in the image of God; and I was created with the freedom to live into that image or away from it. Like the treatment of my alcoholism, what I do with that reality every day is entirely my choice. If I choose to live *away* from that image, then *I* will be at the center of my universe, and my life will be a mess. If I choose to live *into* that image, then *God* will be at the center of my universe, and I can claim my true identity in that center, in God. My sense of that identity will affect the ways in which I relate to all of Creation—to God, myself, other people, other creatures, the environment—everything that makes up the world in which I live. And it can make a world of difference.

IN GOD'S IMAGE

As difficult as we may find it to understand, each of us came from the hand of a God who knew exactly what he was doing when he created us. God had the power to make something else, but he made us, in his own image. When he sent his Son into the world, he made him in *our* earthly image—God made man, the perfect example of man reflecting the image of God—leading the apostle Paul to declare in his second letter to the Corinthians: "And all of us, with unveiled faces, seeing the glory of the Lord as though reflected in a mirror, are being transformed into the same image from one degree of glory to another; for this comes from the Lord, the Spirit" (2 Cor 3:18).

How many people do you know who are totally happy with everything about themselves? Don't most people wish they had a different body or a different set of parents or a different job with less work and more pay? If God created us in God's image, why do we find it so hard to accept with gratitude the way we are? If I want to be other than God created me, I am playing God, instead of playing *with* God, playing the hand that God dealt me.

Not liking the way God created us is the door through which sin entered history. It happened in the Garden of Eden. God created everything exactly as he intended. God placed human-kind in a place of limitless abundance and said in effect: "All of this is yours, all that you need I will give you, and there will always be enough." But instead of trusting God, our human ancestors listened to a serpent, who told them that, if they ate the forbidden fruit, they could be like God, better off than they were—if they would only take control, instead of trusting in God. Adam and Eve had freedom of choice, just as you and I do. They could have said to the serpent: "We don't want to be like God. We are happy being who God created us to be." But they didn't, and we don't. Lack of satisfaction with whom God created us to be opens the door to all kinds of destruction.

Each of us came from the hand of a God who knew exactly what he was doing when he created us.

JUST AS I AM

One of the breakthroughs in my early recovery came when I realized that I was exactly who and where God wanted me to be at that moment. What an enormous relief! I didn't have to try to be or do something else. I could accept with gratitude the way I was. Saying yes to what God created us to be is the way to acceptance and self-fulfillment. This is God's creation. Goodness is to be found in the way the world *is*, as God made it, not as we envision it.

As far back as Jenny could remember, she wanted to be an actor. She acted in school productions beginning in grade school and continuing through high school. She went to college at her local state university, where she majored in theater. Toward the end of her undergraduate career, she received a scholarship to pursue graduate studies in drama at the University of Chicago. While she was in Chicago, the theater department of the university commissioned a new play from a prominent contemporary playwright. Jenny was invited to audition for the lead role in the first production, which she got. She worked very hard for months preparing the part. On opening night, she poured her heart and soul into a performance that was nothing short of brilliant. After thunderous applause and many curtain calls, she was

Goodness is to be found in the way the world is, as God made it, not as we envision it.

sitting in her dressing room, quietly basking in post-performance exhaustion, when there was a knock at the door. She opened it to find standing there a man she did not know. He said: "I wanted to thank you personally for your wonderful performance this evening. I am the author of the play. When I created your role, it was nothing more than a dream. I could only imagine what that role could become. You brought it to life, gave it flesh and blood and breath and energy. You fulfilled my dream for your character. You made my dream a living reality. Thank you."

Someday you and I will meet the Author of our Great Drama, the One who created our role. What will he think of our performance? Will he recognize the role as he conceived it? Like the playwright in the story, God created our role as a dream for us to fulfill. By creating us in his image, God gave us the very best talent. Through thousands of years and countless people, God gave us a very clear script. How we play the role is entirely up to us.

What does it mean to have been created in the image of God? It means literally everything. It is our original birthright. If we live into that image, claiming our true identity in God, we will fulfill God's promise for our life, we will be a true blessing to God's world, and we will find the joy and fullness that come from knowing that we are playing the role that God envisioned and scripted for us. We will be at home in the image of God in us. There is no greater fulfillment.

EIGHT

STANDING ON
HOLY GROUND

S ome went down to the sea in ships,
   doing business on the mighty waters;
they saw the deeds of the LORD,
   his wondrous works in the deep.
For he commanded and raised the stormy wind,
   which lifted up the waves of the sea.
They mounted up to heaven, they went down to the depths;
   their courage melted away in their calamity;
they reeled and staggered like drunkards,
   and were at their wits' end.
Then they cried to the LORD in their trouble,
   and he brought them out from their distress;
he made the storm be still,
   and the waves of the sea were hushed.
Then they were glad because they had quiet,
   and he brought them to their desired haven.

—Psalm 107:23-30

M oses was keeping the flock of his father-in-law Jethro, the priest of Midian; he led his flock beyond the wilderness; and came to Horeb, the mountain of God. There the angel *of the LORD appeared to him in a flame of fire out of a bush; he looked, and the bush was blazing, yet it was not consumed. Then Moses said, "I must turn aside and look at this great sight, and see why the bush is not burned up." When the LORD saw that he had turned aside to see, God called to him out of the bush, "Moses, Moses!" And he said, "Here I am." Then he said, "Come no closer! Remove the sandals from your feet, for the place on which you are standing is holy ground." He said further, "I am the God of your father, the God of Abraham, the God of Isaac, and the God of Jacob." And Moses hid his face, for he was afraid to look at God.*

—Exodus 3:1-6

*O*nce *when Joshua was by Jericho, he looked up and saw a man standing before him with a drawn sword in his hand. Joshua went to him and said to him, "Are you one of us, or one of our adversaries?" He replied, "Neither; but as commander of the army of the LORD I have now come." And Joshua fell on his face to the earth and worshiped, and he said to him, "What do you command your servant, my lord?" The commander of the army of the LORD said to Joshua, "Remove the sandals from your feet, for the place where you stand is holy." And Joshua did so.*

—Joshua 5:13-15

After so many years of feeling as if we didn't "fit" anywhere, not even in our own skin, how could we possibly feel comfortable living without alcohol or drugs in the strange land of recovery? Having taken that decisive step into the unknown, we come to realize with wonder that the strange new land is far better than anything we could imagine. We then discover with joy that it is not just better; it is holy.

—⁓— —⁓— —⁓—

The legendary sports broadcaster Harry Kalas, who was for four decades the voice of the Philadelphia Phillies, once introduced center fielder Garry Maddox with the following words: "He has turned his life around. He used to be depressed and miserable. Now he's miserable and depressed."[1] Sobriety turned my life around, and it was really not so funny. I followed the path of every other alcoholic in recovery: I went to hell and made a U-turn. The journey back has been incredible beyond imagination.

When I first got into recovery, it didn't seem like a very *holy* place. Oh, don't get me wrong, it was infinitely better than the latter days of my active addiction. By the time I hit bottom, I was ready to follow any instruction, if it would relieve my pain. In the image of the psalm that leads this chapter, I had gone "down to the sea" of life in my flimsy ship to do "business on the mighty waters," and I had been tossed around by the tempests of this world until I was at my "wits' end." Finally I had cried to the Lord in my trouble, and the Lord brought me out of my distress to the safe haven of sobriety.

In sobriety I learned that living on the great ocean of life is not about staying in the safe harbor, and it's not about calmer seas. It's about a stronger boat. Being in recovery doesn't gain me some blanket exemption from problems any more than being in an intimate relationship with God gets me membership in some elite club where bad things no longer happen. My program of recovery helps me to build a stronger boat. If my boat is strong enough, it doesn't matter how rough the seas are; I will always make it back to the safe haven. And it's never more than a one-day trip.

Early recovery felt strange, almost too good to be true. The so-called "pink cloud" experienced by many people in early recovery was wonderful, but life still felt awkward. It was as if I were a toddler just learning to walk, which was apt, since this was really the first time that I had ever attempted as an adult to live life on life's terms, as I entered the world beyond active addiction. Gradually the feeling of strangeness gave way to a sense of respect for this way of life. Gradually the feeling of respect gave way to a deepening sense of reverence, then profound awe, as I realized

> *It's not about calmer seas.*
>
> *It's about a stronger boat.*

that I was no longer in the world where I had spent most of my life. Like Moses and Joshua, I was in a holy place, standing on holy ground, surrounded by holiness. And I knew then how Jacob must have felt when he awoke from his dream and said: "Surely the LORD is in this place—and I did not know it!" (Gen 28:16).

THANK GOD I'M AN ALCOHOLIC

One of the strange things about my early recovery was hearing people at meetings say: "I thank God I'm an alcoholic." I thought, *How lame!* This poor person has the same devastating disease I have (note the self-pity), and he's trying to convince himself it's a *good thing!* How bogus is *that?* It reminded me of the time-honored marketing principle for selling products with irreparable flaws. Instead of trying to hide the flaw, try to make people think it's an advantage; the maxim is *if you can't fix it, feature it.* "I thank God I'm an alcoholic." Why would anyone be thankful for such a horrible, irreparable flaw?

> *Many people make it the whole way through life and never have to get real. We're the lucky ones, the chosen ones.*

Today I'm one of those people saying: "I thank God I'm an alcoholic." I'm grateful to be where I am today, with other recovering alcoholics. We live where it's real. People working a program of recovery are some of the most genuine people in this world. Granted we don't have much choice; if we don't stay real, we die. But what a gift! Many people make it the whole way through life and never have to get real. We're the lucky ones, the chosen ones. We get to learn what it means to live authentically out of the core of our divine creation. What an incredible gift!

Some years ago, *Forbes* printed an article about a business owner named Harry Quadracci and his Quad/Graphics printing company, which had an unusual hiring practice. The author of the article described it like this:

> A good many people whom society would dismiss as losers have been given a chance at Quad/Graphics, and they are

grateful. "We hire people who have no education and little direction," Quadracci explains. "They are the kind of people who look at their shoes when they apply for a job. They join the firm not for its high wages—starting salaries on the floor are only about $7.50 an hour—but because we offer them a chance to make something out of themselves."[2]

Like Harry Quadracci, God can build a really successful enterprise using people whom others might dismiss as losers. I was one of those people, staring at my shoes as I applied for a place in the human race. The world didn't think very much of me back then, but God surely did. While I was standing there, staring at my shoes, too ashamed to lift my eyes, God spoke to me out of the burning bushes of my life with the same message delivered to Moses and Joshua: "Take off your shoes. You are standing on holy ground." I've been learning ever since how to live in the midst of that holiness.

The word *holy* has different meanings, but its various ancient roots all have in common a sense of "separateness," being set apart for a special purpose. If you have a Bible, it probably says on it "Holy Bible." It is a book set apart from other books as the Word of God. Israel is called "The Holy Land," the land where God, through Moses and Joshua, led the chosen people out of Egypt and apart from the rest of civilization. Jerusalem is called "The Holy City," set apart by Christians, Jews, and Muslims as the sacred ground of their common ancestry in the patriarch Abraham. Something that is holy has been set aside from common to sacred use.

STANDING ON HOLY GROUND

If we understand *holy* to mean set apart for a special purpose, how then do we understand *holy ground?* The spiritual writer John Mogabgab describes it beautifully:

> Holy ground is the stable place of clarity and confidence in a turbulent human landscape of shifting values, crumbling hopes, frayed trusts, uncertain commitments. Holy ground is the place of life-giving rootedness in something larger than our own lives, something deep enough and enduring enough to keep us anchored and oriented in the storm. Holy ground is the place at once attractive and fearsome, where God speaks and we listen, the place of empowerment, transformation, and sending forth to live victoriously in a world too often disfigured by the defeat of justice, peace, and human dignity, the place where the gracious rule of God is known and the new creation becomes visible, the place where faith can move mountains.[3]

Christian tradition is one of the very few deep religious traditions in which shoes are usually kept on during prayer. Since ancient times, removing one's shoes has been a sign of reverence, humility, vulnerability. Muslims to this day always take off their shoes before they enter a mosque. Sometimes when I lead group prayer, I will invite people to take off their shoes. Taking off our shoes removes an unnatural barrier, a protective layer, allowing us to feel closer to God by feeling closer to the holy ground beneath us.

If you are in recovery, you stand on holy ground. It may not feel or look very holy. Look again. Look around. Look within. You are holy. You have been delivered from the certain death of addiction. You have been set aside for a special purpose. As described by the psalmist, you have been drawn up "from the desolate pit,

If you are in recovery, you stand on holy ground.

out of the miry bog"; your feet have been set "upon a rock" (Ps 40:2). Like Moses and Joshua, you have been led to the Promised Land, the land of new life, the land of recovery. Like Moses and Joshua also, you have an important voice, a story that tells how you got to the holy ground of recovery. Telling your story from the holy ground where you now stand bears strong witness that there is a better way. You are a prophet to those still seeking that way. In the Program, we don't talk about prophets; we call it "sharing our experience, strength, and hope."

Sister Macrina gave voice to this sacred challenge in one of her poems:

> The Moses in my heart trembles
> not quite willing
> to accept the prophet hidden in my being
> wondering how much it will cost
> to allow that prophet to emerge.
>
> O child of unnecessary shoes
> cast them off
> and stand in readiness
> on this holy ground.
> For the Egypt in people's lives
> demands that you see the burning bushes

all around you
aflame
burning wildly
calling you
away from the comfort
of well-protected feet.

The ground you stand on is holy.
Take off your shoes!
The ground of your being is holy.
Take off your shoes!
Awaken your sleeping prophet
Believe in your Moses
and go . . .[4]

"Then Moses said, 'I must turn aside and look at this great sight, and see why the bush is not burned up.' When the LORD saw that he had turned aside to see, God called to him out of the bush . . . ." (Exod 3:3, 4). God did not speak to Moses out of the burning bush until Moses stopped to listen. Pay attention to the burning bushes in your life; there are more of them than you might think. Listen to the voice coming from those burning bushes; it is the voice of God, telling you that you are loved, you are one of a kind, and you have been set aside for a very special purpose. You have been given the precious gift of recovery, to live in that gift and to share it with others. You stand on holy ground. Now take off your shoes!

NINE

LIVING INTO OUR IMPORTANCE

*F or just as the body is one and has many members, and all
the members of the body, though many, are one body, so it
is with Christ. . . . Indeed, the body does not consist of one
member but of many. If the foot would say, "Because I am not
a hand, I do not belong to the body," that would not make it any
less a part of the body. And if the ear would say, "Because I am
not an eye, I do not belong to the body," that would not make it
any less a part of the body. If the whole body were an eye, where
would the hearing be? If the whole body were hearing, where
would the sense of smell be? But as it is, God arranged the members in the body, each one of them, as he chose. If all were a single member, where would the body be? As it is, there are many
members, yet one body.*

—1 Corinthians 12:12, 14-20

Standing on the holy ground of recovery, we experience a growing awareness that we can no longer maintain our self-importance
as the center of our universe. When we come to understand our
true importance in God's world, we begin to live a balanced life
out of our authentic core. At long last, we can feel at home.

—◦◦— —◦◦— —◦◦—

How important are you? It's a question we seldom ask ourselves, and yet our unspoken answer to this unasked question has been a powerful directing force throughout our lives.

Like most addicts, for much of my life I thought I was important. I was special. I played by my own special rules. I knew what I wanted, I wanted it now, and I got frustrated when I didn't get it, often blaming others. Control was essential. If I wasn't in control, someone else was, and that was unacceptable. I had to be in control to get what I wanted. I was the supreme authority in my life.

As my addiction progressed, I was amazed at how many things went wrong with someone as special as me in total control. Eventually the bottom dropped out, in fulfillment of the age-old proverb: "Pride goes before destruction, and a haughty spirit before a fall" (Prov 16:18). I arrived in treatment, devastated and lost, and I came face-to-face with the First Step. Despite all of my special abilities and my control, my life was unmanageable, and I was powerless. Did that mean that I was unimportant? No, I came to learn, it did not; but I was not important in the ways that I used to believe. I was important in ways that were totally different from the self-importance I had felt.

I AM IMPORTANT TO ME

First, I came to understand that I am important to me. I learned that I had to be responsible for myself and that only I could own my recovery. If I was to be worth anything on this earth, I had to step up to the plate and get the help I needed to fix me, because I was the only one I could control. There is a paraphrase of the Serenity Prayer that goes like this: God, grant me serenity to accept the people I cannot change, courage to change the person I can, and wisdom to know that person is me. Jesus said: "Unless a grain of wheat falls into the earth and dies, it

I learned that I had to be responsible for myself and that only I could own my recovery.

remains just a single grain; but if it dies, it bears much fruit" (John 12:24). When I was active in my addiction, I was like that grain of wheat: alone, isolated—often by choice. It was only when the old me died that I, like that grain of wheat, began to bear much fruit. That's a whole different kind of importance.

I AM IMPORTANT TO GOD

Second, I came to understand that I am important to God. God made me in God's own image. I am a child of my Creator. I have the spirit of God in me, as surely as any child has the genetic code of a parent. God doesn't want me to be lost, any more than any loving parent wants to lose a child. Jesus explained it in a parable: "Which one of you, having a hundred sheep and losing one of them, does not leave the ninety-nine in the wilderness and go after the one that is lost until he finds it? When he has found it, he lays it on his shoulders and rejoices.

And when he comes home, he calls together his friends and neighbors, saying to them, 'Rejoice with me, for I have found my sheep that was lost'" (Luke 15:4-6).

God can seem so far away, especially in the isolation of addiction. It's only when we get into recovery and a personal relationship with God that we realize God is not far away. God is right here with us, living in each of us. God weeps with us in our sorrow and dances with us in our joy, just as any loving parent does with a child of his or her creation. In addiction we were like lost sheep. Every Sunday, in the chapel at Cumberland Heights, we sing: "I once was lost but now am found." Imagine God's joy as he laid each of us over his shoulders and carried us back to the fold. That's a whole different kind of importance.

I am important to God.

We are also important to God, because each of us has an important role to play that only we can play in fulfilling God's plan. The apostle Paul, writing to the early church at Corinth, described this in physical terms using as a metaphor the Body of Christ. In Paul's metaphor, each of us is a hand, or an ear, or an eye, or a foot. Each of us is unique; each of us is important; and it takes all of us, with all of our gifts and graces, working together, to make the body function.

In 1990, *The New York Times* ran a story about a nurse in Kansas City by the name of Cheryl Wood. Mrs. Wood lost her paycheck just before Christmas. The check was already endorsed and could have been cashed by anyone who found it. It was found by Rosemary Pritchett, a homeless mother of three children, who had just put a bid with what little money she had on an abandoned house. Mrs. Pritchett said later that it never crossed her mind to cash the check. She looked up Mrs. Wood's phone number from the address printed on the check and used her last quarter to make the call. When Mrs. Wood came to pick up the check, she found the Pritchetts in a homeless shelter and offered a reward. Mrs. Pritchett declined. She asked only for a note of thanks she could show her children. "I wanted the children to know that when you find something, somebody lost it," she explained.

Only when Mrs. Wood threatened to leave the money on the floor and walk away did Mrs. Pritchett accept the reward. The next day Mrs. Pritchett's bid on the abandoned house was accepted, and she moved her children and their few possessions into a house that was little more than a shell. The walls were crumbling, and vandals had torn out the wires and plumbing. A few days later, Mrs. Wood visited and found the Pritchetts trying to repair the house with only a hammer and screwdriver. She decided to do something about the situation. She took up the Yellow Pages, worked her way through the contractor section, and finally found a contractor who agreed to become supervisor without charge. Another contractor offered to install a free water heater, and a supplier built windows and donated fixtures. Mrs. Wood's retired uncle also worked on the restoration. When newspapers and television picked up the story, the project took on a life of its own. Contractors and builders offered free labor and equipment. Debris was removed free of charge, and total strangers came forward to help. In the end, $30,000 worth of labor and equipment was donated.[1] Adjusted for inflation, the figure would be several times that amount today.

If you had asked any one of those people at the outset if this could be achieved, the person probably would have said it was impossible; and, from the perspective of a single person, that probably would have been correct. What they ultimately achieved was a result of everyone working together, doing his or her own small part. The total result was far greater than the sum of the parts. Each one of us has a role to play that is vital to God's plan for this world. That's a whole different kind of importance.

I AM IMPORTANT TO OTHERS

Finally, each one of us is important to others. To me one of the most wonderful aspects of Twelve-Step recovery is the emphasis on service. It's in the Twelfth Step, where we agree to take everything we have learned in our spiritual awakening and share the message with others. After all of our work on ourselves and with

Each one of us is important to others.

God, it's the jumping off point. In order to continue to have what we have in recovery, we must continually give it away. It's like a freshwater spring with an underground source constantly replenishing its supply. The more we give away, the more we have to give. Jesus said it to his disciples: "For those who want to save their life will lose it, and those who lose their life for my sake will find it" (Matt

16:25). We must lose our self-importance in order to gain our real importance.

To me one of the great ironies in this awareness is that fulfill-ment in life comes from emptiness, not fullness. When we are so full of self-centeredness and questing after our own prizes, there's no room in our cup for God's grace. It's only when we empty our-selves that God has space in which to work. Empty we are pure capacity for God. Macrina Wiederkehr, from whose wisdom I have quoted throughout this book, has written a poem about being in that emptiness, both *alone* and *all-one* with God. Part of the poem reads:

> It is a terrible grace.
> An awesome gift,
> But terrifying all the same.
> There is no way to get there
> except to lose yourself,
> to lose what you know of yourself.
> And then, the battle is over.
> There will be nothing left but God.[2]

We must empty ourselves of self-importance, so that God can fill us with his grace and with an understanding of our true importance.

Toward the end of my in-patient treatment, I stepped outside during a break between group sessions. There was a young man there who had been admitted the day before. He was standing by himself, and I went over to strike up a conversation. As I commented on the beautiful day, I hardly expected anything profound in response, but what that young man said to me was one of the most profound things that I learned during my time in treatment. He said: "God made each of us beautiful, but often we can't see that beauty; because God made us not so that we could see our own beauty, but so that others could see it." That's why we're here, not so we can admire our own beauty, but so we can bring beauty into other people's lives. God doesn't work through blinding supernatural spectacles. God works through human beings, and each of us has a unique role to play in accomplishing God's work, in service to others, making God's world more beautiful. That's a whole different kind of importance.

We must lose our self-importance in order to gain our real importance.

A woman had picked up her daughter at school and got her car stuck in the muddy parking lot. The harder she tried to get out, the deeper her wheels sank.

She turned to her little girl and said: "Honey, will you say a prayer and ask God to help us get out of the mud?"

The little girl bowed her head and whispered her request. Just as she raised her head, her mother maneuvered the car easily out of the mud.

"Whatever did you say to God?" the astonished mother asked.

The little girl answered: "I asked God *please* to make you a better driver."

In a simplistic way, this is what our spiritual journey is about. We recall the words of the psalmist: "He raised me out of the miry pit, out of the mud and clay; he set my feet on rock and gave me a firm footing" (Ps 40:2 REB). Once we have been pulled out of the mud and clay of our addiction that keep sucking us down toward death, and our lives have been set on the firm road of recovery, we must spend the rest of our lives learning to be a better driver, because the better driver we are, the better we will be able to fulfill our unique role accomplishing the work that God has given us to do. Our recovery is a gift, given freely in unconditional love. Having accepted this blessed gift, we must do all we can in everything we do to care for ourselves, to help others, and to honor the Giver.

We are truly blessed to be where we are today in each of our journeys of recovery. We have been led to a spiritual awakening that many people never attain, and we have come to understand the humility that must accompany our spiritual awareness. We are indeed important, in ways that we may never have imagined. We were created to do important work that no one else can do, and we have a Higher Power who is with us at every step. Each of us brings to God's world his or her own unique beauty. It's all a gift that has been given to us, and we must spend the rest of our lives giving it away. It's that important.

TEN

LEARNING TO PRAY

I consider that the sufferings of this present time are not worth comparing with the glory about to be revealed to us. . . . For in hope we were saved. Now hope that is seen is not hope. For who hopes for what is seen? But if we hope for what we do not see, we wait for it with patience. Likewise the Spirit helps us in our weakness; for we do not know how to pray as we ought, but that very Spirit intercedes with sighs too deep for words. And God, who searches the heart, knows what is the mind of the Spirit, because the Spirit intercedes for the saints according to the will of God. We know that all things work together for good for those who love God, who are called according to his purpose. . . . What then are we to say about these things? If God is for us, who is against us? He who did not withhold his own Son, but gave him up for all of us, will he not with him also give us everything else? Who will bring any charge against God's elect? It is God who justifies. Who is to condemn? It is Christ Jesus, who died, yes, who was raised, who is at the right hand of God, who indeed intercedes for us.

—Romans 8:18, 24-28, 31-34

Prayer is the most important means of developing a personal relationship with our Higher Power. Though we may experience

God in many ways, nowhere is that experience deeper than in prayer.

—ɯ— —ɯ— —ɯ—

The Gospels record many occasions on which Jesus withdrew from whatever was happening around him so that he could pray. In the Gospel according to Mark, we read: "In the morning, while it was still very dark, he got up and went out to a deserted place, and there he prayed" (Mark 1:35). On another such occasion, Luke tells us that "he was praying in a certain place, and after he had finished, one of his disciples said to him, 'Lord, teach us to pray, as John taught his disciples'" (Luke 11:1). It was a perfectly reasonable request. In Jewish tradition, it was common for a rabbi to formulate short prayers as models for use by his followers. The disciples knew that John the Baptist had done this, and they were looking for similar guidance from *their* teacher. Jesus' response would become the most famous prayer in the history of civilization. We know it as the Lord's Prayer. Churchgoers pray the prayer during most services; those of us in recovery pray it at the end of every meeting of AA and other 12-Step programs. How many of us, however, looking at our personal prayer life, would not welcome an opportunity to say face-to-face to the Master: "Lord, teach me to pray"?

THE LANGUAGE OF SPIRITUALITY

Prayer is central to many religious traditions. More fundamentally, prayer is the language of spirituality. And it's important to make a clear distinction between spirituality and religion. We are born in the Spirit; but we are taught religion. The spiritual story of humanity is at least 70,000 years old, while formal religions have existed for a mere 4,500 years. If religion is a man sitting in church thinking about fishing, spirituality is a man fishing thinking about God. AA wisdom holds that religion is for people who don't want to go to hell; spirituality is for people who have been there. Members of the Fellowship are careful to point out that "AA is not a religion: we can't open the gates of heaven and let you in, but we can open the gates of hell and let you out." If organized religion helps your recovery, use it to the extent that it helps; if it doesn't help, you don't need it.

Prayer is central to recovery. There are prayers associated with both the Third and Seventh Steps; the Eleventh Step encourages "prayer and meditation"; and there are five things that we are told we must do every day for our sobriety: (1) begin the day on our knees, asking God to keep us sober that day (God loves to answer knee-mail); (2) read from the literature; (3) talk to another alcoholic or addict; (4) go to a meeting; and (5) end the day on our knees, thanking God for keeping us clean and sober that day. Of the five things, two of them are prayer—that's 40 percent, compared with 20 percent for each of the other three things. Prayer is vitally important to recovery, but how much do we really understand about prayer? How do we do it? What can we expect from it?

We are born in the Spirit; but we are taught religion.

I grew up in the church. Prayer was a part of my life, not necessarily a big part, but I was familiar with it. At times I even did it daily, but no one ever taught me to pray. I thought prayer was about talking *to* God, giving God instructions, praying *for* things that I wanted, as if God were some sort of cosmic bellhop just waiting for my orders. I wanted to serve God, but only in an advisory capacity.

The late comedian Flip Wilson had a character named Reverend Leroy, from the Church of What's Happenin' Now, who used to say: "I'm gonna pray now; anybody want anything?" That's sort of what I did. When I didn't get what I wanted, I assumed that God wasn't listening or didn't care or simply had refused my request. Sometimes I tested God: "God, if this is supposed to happen, give me a sign." Sometimes I bargained with God, using the age-old "foxhole prayer": "God, if you just get me out of this mess, I promise _____" (we can all fill in our own blank). I envisioned God way out there somewhere, maybe up in heaven, but in any case far away from wherever I was. I used to pray mostly at night, sometimes in the morning, rarely during the day. It was as

> *I kept launching my prayers heavenward, hoping that somehow they might hit their mark, when I should have been turning inward, where God lives at the center of my being.*

if I thought God had office hours. As I look back on it, my relationship with God really wasn't much of a relationship.

Today my understanding of prayer is very different. For one thing, I know now that I was looking for God in the wrong place. I kept launching my prayers heavenward, hoping that somehow they might hit their mark, when I should have been turning inward, where God lives at the center of my being. I was searching for God, not realizing that God had always been reaching out to me, and all I had to do was reach back to make the connec-

To speak of man's search for God is like speaking of the mouse's search for the cat.

—C. S. Lewis

tion. There is a famous portrayal of this in Michelangelo's mural of the Creation on the ceiling of the Sistine Chapel in Rome. In the artist's depiction, God is reaching down, while Adam reaches up, their fingertips almost touching. C. S. Lewis once wrote: "To speak of man's search for God is like speaking of the mouse's search for the cat."[1] I never have to search for God. All I have to do is turn toward him and take his already extended hand.

NO PRAYER GOES UNANSWERED

Something else I've learned is that every prayer is heard, and no prayer goes unanswered. Jesus told his disciples: "Whatever you ask for in prayer, believe that you have received it, and it will be yours" (Mark 11:24). In response to the request to teach them to pray, after Jesus had taught his disciples the Lord's Prayer, he went on to tell a parable, which he then summarized by saying: "Ask, and it will be given you; search, and you will find; knock, and the door will be opened for you. For everyone who asks receives, and everyone who searches finds, and for everyone who knocks, the door will be opened" (Luke 11:9-10). These are strong assurances. From the rich Jewish tradition of storytelling comes this personal account of a Hasidic rabbi:

> At the Western Wall in Jerusalem I saw a blind man being led to the wall. He felt the stones with his fingertips, applied a gentle kiss to the sacred stones, and began speaking to God. Although he spoke very rapidly, I could catch some of the words. He was relating to God various things that had happened to him, and some of his requests. At one point he stopped abruptly, "Oh, I'm sorry," he said, "I already told you that yesterday." The sincerity of the man's prayer was electrifying. He had no doubt whatever that what he had said yesterday had been heard by God.[2]

Sometimes God requires our help in answering our own prayers. There is a story about a young man who aspired to be a physician. Every night he prayed: "God, I want to be a doctor; please make me a doctor." One night, after months of this daily petition, he had just finished his prayers, when the stillness of his room was shattered by a booming voice, which said: "Go to medical school!"

Often God answers our prayers through other people. There is a familiar story set in an area of the country that had been ravaged by terrible flooding. People were fleeing for their lives with whatever few possessions they could salvage. As the flood waters rose, one man retreated to the roof of his house. Eventually, as he stood waist-deep in the rising tide, a boat approached. One of the men in the boat threw him a rope and shouted to him to grab onto it, so that he could be pulled to safety. The man on the roof smiled and waved them off, saying: "Thanks anyway. God will take care of me." The men in the boat shook their heads in bewilderment and left. Later, as the water rose above his shoulders, a helicopter stopped to hover overhead, and a man dropped a rope ladder, shouting for the man on the roof to grab onto it so that he could be hoisted to safety. The man smiled and waved them off, saying: "No thanks. God will take care of me." The helicopter flew away. The water continued to rise, and the man drowned. He arrived in heaven and came to stand before God. He was angry and dumbfounded that God could have abandoned him and allowed him to die.

> *Any illusion I may have that my prayers are not being heard or answered is grounded in my limited expectations, not in God's limitless response.*

He confronted God in his anger and said: "How could you do this to me? You told me you would take care of me." God responded: "What were you waiting for? I sent you a lifeboat and a helicopter." God answers prayer in ways that are beyond our imagination. Any illusion I may have that my prayers are not being heard or answered is grounded in my limited expectations, not in God's limitless response.

While all prayer is answered, sometimes we may not like the answer we get. There is the tale of a man who was hiking in a remote area out West and came to the edge of a deep canyon. As he stood peering over the edge of the precipice, he lost his balance and plunged headlong over the edge. Clawing the air frantically as he plummeted to his apparently imminent death, about halfway down he suddenly felt his hands grab onto a branch protruding from the face of the canyon wall, which abruptly stopped his descent. As he hung there, clinging to the branch with both hands, he looked around to find a way out of his predicament. Except for the branch, there was nothing on the sheer face of rock that would offer any foothold. There was no way out. He was stranded, miles from civilization, with no other hikers in the area. He looked to the canyon floor hundreds of feet below. Then he looked up and began to cry for help. "Is anybody up there?" he screamed. As the echo of his own voice died out deep in the canyon, he heard a voice from heaven, and the voice said: "Have faith. Let go of the branch." He looked down again, then looked up and shouted: "Anybody else up there?" Whether we like the answer or not, it will always come, and we can live in the expectation of the psalmist: "But as for me, my prayer is to you, O LORD. At an acceptable time, O God, in the abundance of your steadfast love, answer me" (Ps 69:13).

BE STILL AND LISTEN

I was also amazed to learn that prayer is as much listening as it is speaking. The great nineteenth-century Danish theologian Søren Kierkegaard wrote: "A man prayed, and at first he thought that prayer was talking. But he became more and more quiet until in the end he realized that prayer is listening."[3] When I think about it now, I can't imagine a relationship with *anyone* in which I would do all the talking. Communication is a two-way process. It's a dialogue, not a monologue. It's both speaking and listening. How can I expect to have a relationship with God if I never listen? God created us with two ears and one mouth; I think that was intentional. Babies learn to speak only *after* they have listened for a long time. In order to listen, we have to stop talking. The psalmist wrote: "Be still, and know that I am God!" (Ps 46:10). The sixteenth-century Spanish mystic Saint John of the Cross put it another way: "The Father spoke one Word, which was his Son, and this Word he speaks always in eternal silence, and in silence must it be heard by the soul."[4] Thomas Keating, one of the founders of the modern centering prayer movement, summarized it simply: "Silence is God's first language; everything else is a poor translation."[5]

As a species we are afraid of silence. Our lives are filled with so much noise, activity, clutter. We measure success by achievements. In our culture, we are often much more comfortable as human *doings*, than we are as human *beings*. In all of our doing, we think we are accomplishing so much, when we are actually limiting our spirituality. Eugene Peterson, a professor of spiritual theology and author of the popular Bible translation *The Message*, maintains: "Busyness is the enemy of spirituality. It is essentially laziness! It is doing the easy thing instead of the hard thing. It is filling our time with our own actions instead of paying attention to God."[6]

We recall the familiar story of the sisters Martha and Mary of Bethany, who welcomed Jesus into their home. While Martha bustled around with the tasks of hospitality, Mary sat at the Lord's feet and listened to what he was saying. Eventually Martha came to Jesus and said essentially what a child might whine to a parent: "She's not doing her share." Jesus responded: "Martha, Martha, you are worried and distracted by many things; there is need of only one thing. Mary has chosen the better part, which will not be taken away from her" (Luke 10:41, 42). It's so much easier for us to be Martha, justifying our obsessive busyness by what we think is expected of us; but today, as in the first century, it is Mary, listening in attentive silence at the feet of her Lord, who has the better part.

Prayer is as much listening as it is speaking.

A prominent spiritual writer recalled a poignant, private exchange. He was hard at work in his study one morning, when his four-year-old daughter quietly slipped in, still in her nightgown, and without saying anything climbed up into his lap and laid her head on his shoulder. He said to her: "I'm really glad to see you. What can I do for you? What do you want?" She paused for a moment and then said: "Nothing. I just wanted to be close to you, that's all." That's what it's like simply to *be* in the loving presence of God, to say to God: "Lord, right now I don't want anything; I just want to feel close to you." Silence is an essential part of prayer.

LIVING IN THE PRESENCE OF GOD

We live in our false selves, a collection of masks designed to protect us from hurt and to project to others the ways in which we want them to see us. In deep silence, in the presence of God, all of this falls away. In silence, we must meet ourselves face-to-face, at the center, without the masks. It's scary, it's lonely at first, it's pure, and it's where God lives in each one of us.

There is an ancient image, originating with the so-called Desert Fathers and Mothers of the fourth through sixth centuries that likens our soul to a bucket of water reflecting the Light of God. When the water gets murky with the impurities of our lives, it doesn't reflect God's light very well. In deep prayer, in the pure presence of God, our impurities gradually settle out, leaving our soul clear to reflect the Light of God. It is in that place of communion with God where the layers of our false self fall away, revealing the pure state of our creation, before we constructed an alternative scenario that never really existed.

The hole in our soul is a God-shaped hole.

It can also be helpful to imagine ourselves with a hollow center. Spiritual writers and psychotherapists sometimes call it the "hole in the soul," a term invented by the seventeenth-century French mathematician and philosopher Blaise Pascal. It's like a chocolate cream in which someone forgot to put the creamy center. In us, however, it's not a mistake; it's not a defect. In the fourth century, Saint Augustine prayed: "You have made us for

yourself, O God, and our hearts are restless until they rest in you."
God intentionally made us with the "hole in the soul" so that we
would turn to him to fill that emptiness. The hole, our spiritual
emptiness, is the source of our yearning for God, but God left it
to us to figure that out. How many years do we spend trying to fill
that hole with alcohol, drugs, sex, food, relationships, money,
material possessions, before finally figuring out that it's a God-
shaped hole? It's only when we go to that center and empty ourselves of everything that doesn't fit that we find ourselves in the
presence of God, who fills the emptiness and makes us whole.
Prayer is how we get there.

THE DIVINE CENTER

This type of deep prayer has been understood for many hundreds of years. Its origins stretch to the roots of monasticism in
the fourth century, and it has seen an enthusiastic revival in the
last thirty years. Today we call it *contemplative prayer,* and there
are many techniques—such as *centering prayer*—used in its practice. No matter what techniques are used, the goal is the same: to
turn inward to the center, not to *do* anything, but simply to *be* in
the presence of God. Thomas Merton, one of the most prominent
spiritual voices of the twentieth century, expressed it powerfully:
"The fact is . . . that if you descend into the depths of your own
spirit . . . and arrive somewhere near the center of what you *are,*
you are confronted with the inescapable truth that, at the very
root of your existence, you are in constant and immediate and
inescapable contact with the infinite power of God."[7] Writing in

the early 1940s, a Quaker named Thomas Kelly described it no less profoundly:

> Deep within us all there is an amazing inner sanctuary of the soul, a holy place, a Divine Center, a speaking Voice, to which we may continuously return. Eternity is at our hearts, pressing upon our time-torn lives, warming us with intimations of an astounding destiny, calling us home unto Itself. Yielding to these persuasions, gladly committing ourselves in body and soul, utterly and completely, to the Light Within, is the beginning of true life. It is a dynamic center, a creative Life that presses to birth within us. It is a Light Within which illumines the face of God and casts new shadows and new glories upon the face of men. It is a seed stirring to life if we do not choke it. It is the Shekinah [i.e., a visible manifestation of a divine presence] of the soul, the Presence in the midst. Here is the Slumbering Christ, stirring to be awakened, to become the soul we clothe in earthly form and action. And He is within us all.[8]

Kelly's description takes us beyond the technique of prayer to the place of prayer in our lives. I was always puzzled by the references in Scripture to constant prayer. Jesus advocated praying "always" (Luke 18:1); the Apostle Paul, in his first letter to the early Christians at Thessalonika, admonished them to "pray without ceasing" (1 Thess 5:17). I always thought that was a bit impractical. If you pray all

To live prayerfully is to live gratefully, . . . to feel at home in God's world.

the time, how do you get anything else done? Once again I had missed the point. Prayer is not only about prayers; in fact, prayers can be an obstacle to prayer. True prayer is not an activity; it is a way of life. To live prayerfully is to live gratefully, to be able to see the holiness that surrounds us, to feel at home in God's world. To live prayerfully is to know that calm center, where we can *be* purely in the dynamic presence of God, and to know that it is always there, day and night, within us, within reach.

TRANSFORMED IN THE PRESENCE

Prayer changes things. Prayer changes us. Prayer places us in a presence in which we are miraculously transformed. In that presence, our painful loneliness becomes glorious solitude; our restless senses become a restful spirit; our outward-reaching craving becomes an inward-reaching searching; our fearful clinging becomes fearless play; our impatient desire for having becomes patient listening for being. In that presence, our false self, with all our character defects, gradually falls away, leaving our true self, in all its purity and wholeness; and we become one with God. In that place, we also come to see the path that God has set before us. When the winds that buffet our lives obscure the path with the scattered leaves of our worldly distractions, we have simply and gently to brush them aside to the edge of our consciousness in order to see the path clearly once again. No matter how hectic life gets, we can always reach in and touch our center, and once again feel instantly and totally at home in God's world. We don't have to retreat to a cloistered community to find such peace. Through prayer, and a prayerful life, we can find it anywhere, in the midst of anything. Once again, Sister Macrina expressed it beautifully in poetry:

> the quiet in me smiled on my noise
> the slow in me smiled on my hurry
> and my life miracled into
> a calm on the lake.
>
> Jesus woke up in my boat
> without my asking
> and commanded the winds
> to subside.
>
> I was asked not to run away
> from my noise and hurry
> but to enter it
> and embrace it most gently.
>
> it was at the moment
> of my entering
> that I felt the miracle.
>
> the quiet in me smiled on my noise
> the slow in me smiled on my hurry
> and my life miracled into
> a calm on the lake.[9]

PRACTICE MAKES BETTER

The practice of prayer is just that: practice. There is no getting it right. No one has ever done it perfectly. In life, as in the

Program, we claim spiritual progress, rather than spiritual perfection. No matter how difficult it may seem at times, however, we must never stop trying. The words of the apostle Paul can become our mantra for daily living: "Rejoice in hope, be patient in suffering, persevere in prayer" (Rom 12:12). The beauty in this life is in the journey. Prayer can transform that journey from a tedious test of endurance into a wonderful pilgrimage of discovery. How we practice prayer makes a difference in who we are and in who we will become. There is nothing that doesn't belong in prayer. All of life must get into our prayers, and prayer must spill into all of life. Prayer is not a pious adornment of life; it is the very essence of life. Practice does not make perfect. Practice makes better, and a better prayer life will lead to a better life in every way imaginable.

A Prayer for Solitude

Lord, teach us to pray, as you taught your disciples so long ago. Help us to know that your Spirit, with sighs too deep for words, is always praying within us, and we have simply to join in that prayer. Help us to find that deserted place within us, that stillness in which we are one with you, and from which we can see the holiness that surrounds us and the path that you have set before us. With the assurance that you answer all our prayers, grant us the patience to wait in silence for the answers, the wisdom to understand the answers when they come, and the grace to accept them with gratitude. Amen.

ELEVEN

CARING FOR
OUR ANGER

*T*hen the Pharisees went and plotted to entrap him in what he said. So they sent their disciples to him, along with the Herodians, saying, "Teacher, we know that you are sincere, and teach the way of God in accordance with truth, and show deference to no one; for you do not regard people with partiality. Tell us, then, what you think. Is it lawful to pay taxes to the emperor, or not?" But Jesus, aware of their malice, said, "Why are you putting me to the test, you hypocrites? Show me the coin used for the tax." And they brought him a denarius. Then he said to them, "Whose head is this, and whose title?" They answered, "The emperor's." Then he said to them, "Give therefore to the emperor the things that are the emperor's, and to God the things that are God's." When they heard this, they were amazed; and they left him and went away.

—Matthew 22:15-22

Life in recovery is marked by ongoing discernment of our character defects and readiness for God to remove them. No other character defect is as destructive as anger and all its related emotions.

—///— —///— —///—

The story appeared in the *Chicago Tribune*. According to the report, a man and a woman were driving a van in the far left lane of Chicago's Northwest Tollway. In back were their two small children. A white Cadillac driven by an ex-convict suddenly pulled up behind them, tailgating mere inches from their bumper. The man driving the van slowed down. The driver of the Cadillac pulled into the right lane, passed the van, and then swerved suddenly back in front of the van, so suddenly that the van driver had to swerve to avoid a collision. The Cadillac sped away. The van driver accelerated and gave chase. He eventually pulled alongside the white Cadillac and reportedly began yelling and screaming. According to a witness, the two men gestured angrily at each other. The driver of the Cadillac then pulled a handgun and fired at the van. The bullet entered the side of the van and hit the baby girl, entering under her left ear and exiting above her right ear. The little girl lived, but she is blind in one eye, half-blind in the other, partially deaf, and suffers severe mental and physical disabilities. The man who fired the gun is in jail. The parents of the little girl now live with the terrible pain of regret. Anger usually escalates—often in horribly tragic ways.

I HAVE TOTAL CONTROL

Anger is the most destructive of all emotions. People have understood this for thousands of years. In the fourth century B.C.E., the Greek philosopher Plato taught about the dangers of anger. Since the time of Gregory the Great in the sixth century C.E., the church has included anger among the so-called "seven deadly sins." Uncontrolled it can erupt into violence. Suppressed it can become a kind of cancer, destroying us from within. The contemporary spiritual writer Frederick Buechner offers this observation:

> Of the seven deadly sins, anger is possibly the most fun. To lick your wounds, to smack your lips over grievances long past, to roll over your tongue the prospect of bitter confrontations still to come, to savor to the last toothsome morsel both the pain you are given and the pain you are giving back—in many ways it is a feast fit for a king. The chief drawback is that what you are wolfing down is yourself. The skeleton at the feast is you.[1]

The Big Book calls anger a "dubious luxury of normal men" that is, however, "poison" for the alcoholic.[2]

The irony in all of this is that my anger is not about the people or circumstances that I think *cause* my anger. My anger is about me. I have total control over it. No one or no thing can *make* me angry unless I allow it, unless I willingly give up my control. This crucial understanding is poignantly illustrated by the story of a man who purchased a newspaper at a newsstand. He greeted the newsman very courteously, but in return received gruff and discourteous service. Accepting the newspaper, which was rudely shoved in his face, the customer politely smiled and wished the newsman a nice weekend. A friend observed all of this and asked, "Does he always treat you so rudely?"

"Yes, unfortunately he does."

"And are you always so polite and friendly to him?"

"Yes, I am."

"Why are you so nice to him when he is so rude to you?"

"Because I don't want *him* to decide how *I* am going to act."

No one or no thing can make me angry unless I allow it, unless I willingly give up my control.

What an empowering realization: I have total control over my anger. But now what do I do with it? If I accept that anger is a reality of life—indeed a gift from God—how can I be attentive to my anger, so that it can be a source of good in my life, rather than a force of destruction? How can I care for my anger so that its energy can be a positive force encouraging my spiritual formation, rather than an obstacle separating me from God, myself, and others?

GOOD ANGER

Not all anger is bad. Anger is, after all, a natural part of who we are, as God made us. The Bible is full of anger. In the Old Testament, we see time and again the wrath of God directed against his unfaithful people. (You may remember that once he even wiped out all but one family with a flood. Now *that's* some serious anger!) Many people have found this unfortunately generalized image of a vindictive God to be a formidable barrier in their desire to develop a personal relationship with an understanding and compassionate Higher Power.

In the New Testament, Jesus brought to human form the image of a loving God. The author John Killinger, who spent twenty-five years of his distinguished career on the faculty of Vanderbilt Divinity School, asserts that Jesus was God's answer to a bad reputation. As a human being, however, Jesus got angry. All four Gospels record the occasion when he went up to Jerusalem and found in the temple people selling cattle, sheep, and doves, and money changers seated at their tables (Matt 21:12, 13; Mark 11:15, 16; Luke 19:45, 46; John 2:14, 16). Reacting in anger, he fashioned a whip out of cords and drove them all out, shouting: "Stop making my Father's house a marketplace!" On another occasion, upon entering the synagogue on the Sabbath, he found a man with a withered hand. The Pharisees stood by, waiting to see if Jesus would heal the man, so that they could accuse him of breaking the Law by doing work on the Sabbath. According to Mark's Gospel, Jesus "looked around at them with anger; he was grieved at their hardness of heart and said to the man, 'Stretch out your hand.' He stretched it out, and his hand was restored" (Mark 3:5). Used appropriately, anger can be a good—even healing—thing.

THE REAL PROBLEM

A close reading of the Bible reveals that the problem is not anger, but rather how we care for our anger. In the Hebrew Wisdom Literature of the Old Testament, there is much good advice on the subject. The book of Proverbs addresses various aspects of anger, as shown in these five different passages:

- "A man of quick temper acts foolishly" (14:17a RSV).
- "Whoever is slow to anger has great understanding, but one who has a hasty temper exalts folly" (14:29).
- "One who is slow to anger is better than the mighty, and one whose temper is controlled than one who captures a city" (16:32).
- "Those with good sense are slow to anger, and it is their glory to overlook an offense" (19:11).
- "For as pressing milk produces curds, and pressing the nose produces blood, so pressing anger produces strife" (30:33).

In Ecclesiastes, another Wisdom book, we read: "Do not be quick to anger, for anger lodges in the bosom of fools" (Eccl 7:9).

The problem is not getting angry. The problem is staying angry, clinging to that anger as it grows into a resentment.

The teaching of Jesus most often cited as a condemnation of anger appears in the Sermon on the Mount. In what is undoubtedly a compilation of many teachings of Jesus, we read: "You have heard that it was said to those of ancient times, 'You shall not murder'; and 'whoever murders shall be liable to judgment.' But I say to you that if you are angry with a brother or sister, you will be liable to judgment; and if you insult a brother or sister, you will be liable to the council; and if you say, 'You fool,' you will be liable to the hell of fire" (Matt 5:21, 22). Many interpreters have claimed a literal reading of this passage, which would indicate that not only is it sinful to get angry with someone, it is as serious a sin as murdering that person. If we look behind the most widely circulated English translations to the original Greek text, we learn that the form of the verb used here for being angry is a present participle, denoting continuous action. A more accurate translation would be "if you are *continuously* angry with a brother or sister." The problem is not *getting* angry. The problem is *staying* angry, clinging to that anger as it grows into a resentment. Now we are firmly within the canon of Alcoholics Anonymous.

RESENTMENT

The Big Book could not be more explicit: "Resentment is the number one offender. It destroys more alcoholics than anything else."[3] It is not our anger that poisons us; it is our obsessive clinging to the wrongs of the past that holds us prisoner *in* the past and prevents us from living productively in the present or grasping happiness in the future. A former inmate of a Nazi concentration camp was visiting a friend who had been a fellow prisoner. "Have you forgiven the Nazis?" he asked his friend.

"Yes."

"Well, I haven't. I'm still consumed with hatred for them."

"In that case," said his friend gently, "they still have you in prison."

Resentment is the antithesis of spirituality. It may be directed at others, but it hurts most deeply the person who holds it; in fact, harboring resentment has been likened to swallowing poison and waiting for someone else to die. Resentment focuses on self as victim. Instead of seeing others through eyes of love and compassion, we become blinded by their deficiencies. Obsessed with *their* past faults and failings, we lose sight of *our own* present defects and shortcomings. If we are ever to relate to others with tolerance, acceptance, and compassion, we must begin by recognizing and coming to peace with our own imperfection.

> *Harboring resentment has been likened to swallowing poison and waiting for someone else to die.*

It is only in our own brokenness that we can relate to the brokenness of others. It is only in our own woundedness that we can reach out and touch the woundedness of others in meaningful ways. Even though we may have been innocent in a particular situation, we have all made serious enough mistakes in other situations that none of us can ever afford to say: "I am an innocent person, unlike this sinner I am dealing with." God created us with all of our wonderful imperfections precisely so that we could never be self-sufficient; we would always need both God and each other in order to survive in this world.

SEPARATION FROM GOD

The most tragic consequence of prolonged anger is that it separates us from God. Many theologians define sin as anything that separates us from God. Anger certainly fits the definition. The story is told of the time when Leonardo da Vinci was working on his painting *The Last Supper* and became angry with a certain man. Losing his temper, he lashed out at the other fellow with bitter words. Returning to his canvas, Leonardo attempted to work on the face of Jesus but was so upset he could not compose himself for the painstaking work. Finally he put down his tools and sought out the subject of his wrath and asked his forgiveness. The man accepted his

It is impossible for us to see the face of God in our life, when all we can see are the faces of people with whom we are angry.

apology, and Leonardo was able to return to his workshop and finish painting the face of Jesus. Just as Leonardo could not see the face of Jesus through his anger, it is impossible for us to see the face of God in our life, when all we can see are the faces of people with whom we are angry.

NEVER GO TO BED ANGRY

Another lesson that we can learn from Leonardo is to deal with our anger in the present. Resist the temptation to drag it with us into the future, as it grows from anger into resentment, or possibly even hatred. Followers of the apostle Paul offered this advice to the early Christians at Ephesus: "Be angry but do not sin; do not let the sun go down on your anger . . . ." (Eph 4:26).

In other words, resolve your anger before the sun goes down, so that you can sleep in peace and greet the blessings of tomorrow without the baggage of today. It is for good reason that the Tenth Step advises us to admit our discerned wrongdoings *promptly*.

In the Gospel account that heads this chapter, Jesus provides a marvelous example of how to deal with present anger in the face of obvious malice. In the story, the Pharisees (a sect of self-proclaimed orthodox Jews) attempt first to set him up with smooth words, pretending to appreciate his honesty. Then they seek to entrap him with their question: Is it lawful to pay taxes to Caesar? If Jesus says no, he appears to be subversive of the Roman state; if he says yes, he seems to collaborate with the Romans, who were a foreign occupying force. Seeing through the trick, Jesus seizes neither of the alternatives presented. Instead he confronts the Pharisees with their malice and their true motive of trying to trap him. "You hypocrites! Why are you putting me to the test?" We should note that, in the face of this concealed hostility, Jesus neither retreats from his assailants nor retaliates in kind. Nor does he discuss the question on the terms in which the Pharisees present it. He first simply names the question for what it is, a malicious attack, and he deals with it in the present, then moves on to other things.

Caring for Our Anger

Recognizing anger as an important reality of life, how do we care for our anger—without savoring it, denying it, or diverting it into sarcasm, nagging, or more subtle, spiteful behaviors? The first thing I think we must do is to make space for our anger, someplace where we can sit *with* our anger, rather than *on* it. Whether that be mental space or actual physical space, we need to create a place where we can examine our anger attentively and carefully. The Vietnamese Buddhist monk Thich Nhat Hanh offers this insight:

> When we are angry, we are not usually inclined to return to ourselves. We want to think about the person who is making us angry, to think about his hateful aspects: his rudeness, dishonesty, cruelty . . . and so on. The more we think about him, listen to him, or look at him, the more our anger flares. His dishonesty and hatefulness may be real, imaginary, or exaggerated, but in fact the root of the problem is the anger itself, and we have to come back and look first of all inside ourselves. . . . Like a fireman, we have to pour water on the blaze first and not waste time looking for the one who set the house on fire.[4]

Second, we need to take our anger to God. We need to speak our anger truthfully to God, to tell God what we are actually thinking and feeling, resisting the temptation merely to brood over our anger in God's presence. Taking our anger honestly to God in prayer will help us humble ourselves, so that we can then accept God's help.

Finally, we need to offer to God the source of our anger. If that is a situation, ask God for guidance in handling it. If the source of our anger is a person, offer that person to God for God's blessing. Meditate in prayer on the ways in which vulnerabilities and weaknesses of your own life make you much more *like* than *unlike* the person with whom you are angry. The modern spiritual writer Glenn Hinson expresses beautifully this profound dynamic:

Rather than asking God to side with us in our battle or at least to remain neutral while we beat up on the other person, prayer *for* another means to bring that person, just as he or she is, with ourselves before God so the rays of God's transforming love can pour over both of us, to transform and renew and redirect. Prayer is about love. In prayer we open ourselves to the love of God. We push open our doors and fling back our shutters and let God's love flood our inner chambers like the sun's rays flood a dark room.[5]

The program of Alcoholics Anonymous offers sage advice in this important area:

When some hurting person approaches an A.A. sponsor or friend to complain of being victimized or to moan that he cannot get rid of a resentment because he feels unable to forgive, the usual advice, judiciously offered, runs: "Well, I'd say, Pray for the son of a bitch!" And astounding as it may sound to the outsider, it works! Time after time at meetings of Alcoholics Anonymous, experiences of forgiveness are detailed in just such stories.

I just *couldn't* forgive the *&%#, but my sponsor said "Pray for the s.o.b.," and I did, and would you believe it, one day I realized that I no longer felt resentful . . . somehow, the whole thing just didn't bother me anymore![6]

This is not rocket science or voodoo psychology; it is simply God working in the lives of people who ask for God's help. It is God doing for us what we cannot do for ourselves.

Words from the early church resound on this point across nearly two thousand years. In the Epistle of James we read: "You must understand this, my beloved: Let everyone be quick to listen, slow to speak, slow to anger; for your anger does not produce God's righteousness" (1:19, 20). In a wonderful summary of the apostle Paul's teaching, one of his followers wrote to the Colossians:

> But now you must get rid of all such things—anger, wrath, malice, slander, and abusive language from your mouth. . . . As God's chosen ones, holy and beloved, clothe yourselves with compassion, kindness, humility, meekness, and patience. Bear with one another and, if anyone has a complaint against another, forgive each other; just as the Lord has forgiven you, so you also must forgive. Above all, clothe yourselves with love, which binds everything together in perfect harmony. And let the peace of Christ rule in your hearts, to which indeed you were called in the one body. (3:8, 12-15a)

As children of God, we are all part of one body. Each one of us, with all of our individual gifts and graces and weaknesses, is needed in order to make the body of humankind whole. It has been said that the truth is not in any one of us; it is between us. We cannot bring to each other our little piece of the truth if we are separated by anger.

WE NEED EACH OTHER

Some years ago, the Seattle Special Olympics provided the setting for an inspirational life lesson. People who were there are still telling the story. A group of children, each one challenged in some way, lined up to begin a race. The starting gun went off, and they all began to "race" for the finish line. Struggling to run as fast as he could, one little boy tripped and fell, tumbling head over heels several times on the track. One of the little girls in the race realized what had happened, stopped running, and walked back to where the little boy was sitting on the track crying. She leaned down to him, kissed him gently on the cheek, and told him that it would be all right. One by one, the other participants stopped and walked back to where the boy was sitting. Several of them helped him to his feet. They formed a line with their arms around each other's shoulders, and they walked, supporting each other, crossing the finish line together, each one a winner. The standing ovation of the crowd lasted for more than ten minutes.

The truth is not in any one of us; it is between us.

According to AA wisdom: "You alone can do it, but you cannot do it alone." None of us can do it alone. With all of our imperfections, we need God and we need each other to make a whole creation. How much more we could accomplish if we would stop *competing* with each other and work instead at *completing* each other, reaching out in love rather than hatred, in forgiveness rather than vengeance, supporting each other as we walk arm-in-arm toward the same finish line. Only if we learn to care for our anger will this be possible.

TWELVE

GRANTING AND ACCEPTING FORGIVENESS

*T*hen Peter came and said to him, "Lord, if another member of the church sins against me, how often should I forgive? As many as seven times?" Jesus said to him, "Not seven times, but, I tell you, seventy-seven times. For this reason the kingdom of heaven may be compared to a king who wished to settle accounts with his slaves. When he began the reckoning, one who owed him ten thousand talents was brought to him; and, as he could not pay, his lord ordered him to be sold, together with his wife and children and all his possessions, and payment to be made. So the slave fell on his knees before him, saying, 'Have patience with me, and I will pay you everything.' And out of pity for him, the lord of that slave released him and forgave him the debt. But that same slave, as he went out, came upon one of his fellow slaves who owed him a hundred denarii; and seizing him by the throat, he said, 'Pay what you owe.' Then his fellow slave fell down and pleaded with him, 'Have patience with me, and I will pay you.' But he refused; then he went and threw him into prison until he would pay the debt. When his fellow slaves saw what had happened, they were greatly distressed, and they went and reported to their lord all that had taken place. Then his lord summoned him and said to him, 'You wicked slave! I forgave you all that debt because you pleaded with me. Should you*

not have had mercy on your fellow slave, as I had mercy on you?'
And in anger his lord handed him over to be tortured until he would
pay his entire debt. So my heavenly Father will also do to every one
of you, if you do not forgive your brother or sister from your heart."
—Matthew 18:21-35

Forgiveness can be a very effective antidote to anger; however, while caring for our anger remains a lifelong challenge, forgiveness—at its various levels—can seem at times nearly impossible. How can we learn to both give and receive forgiveness?

—w— —w— —w—

"Forgiveness is a mystery. It belongs to the realm of freedom rather than the realm of necessity; it is scented with the spices of grace rather than the sweat of legalism; it delights and humbles with the impact of wholly unexpected bounty; gentler than a tender embrace, it is tougher than the bands of retribution that strap us tightly to our pain."[1] These words of the contemporary spiritual writer John Mogabgab set before us one of the most difficult challenges of being human: the challenge of giving and receiving forgiveness. We can choose to ignore the challenge, both to forgive and to accept forgiveness. We can choose to carry resentments through all of our life on earth. We can choose to believe that we are unworthy of being forgiven. But unless we can both receive and grant forgiveness, we will never be able to live into the fullness of our creation, nor will we ever be at peace with ourselves, our world, or our God.

Forgiveness is at the heart of every significant religious, philosophical, ethical, and psychological construct. Forgiveness certainly stands at the heart of the Christian life—God's forgiveness of us and our forgiveness of others, ourselves, and God. Forgiveness is also at the heart of recovery. Anyone who has worked the Eighth and Ninth Steps has faced this squarely. The concept is not new. Since ancient Hebrew times, forgiveness has been understood as the root of happiness, as witnessed in the words of the psalmist: "Happy are those whose transgression is forgiven, whose sin is covered" (Ps 32:1). Reconciliation—mutual forgiveness—is one of the seven sacraments of the universal Christian church; indeed, for professing Christians forgiveness is an absolute requirement.

Jesus taught that we cannot even approach God if we are not at peace with others. Remember his dramatic instruction in the Sermon on the Mount: "When you are offering your gift at the altar, if you remember that your brother or sister has something against you, leave your gift there before the altar and go; first be reconciled to your brother or sister, and then come and offer your gift" (Matt 5:23, 24). The apostle Paul and his followers wrote frequently and at great length about the application of forgiveness to everyday life. We come to the heart of the matter in the Epistle to the Ephesians, probably written by one or more followers of Paul in the years following his death: "Put away from you all bitterness and wrath and anger and wrangling and slander, together with all malice, and be kind to one another, tenderhearted, forgiving one another, as God in Christ has forgiven you" (Eph 4:31, 32).

The author's closing words, "forgiving one another, as God in Christ has forgiven you," echo the words of Jesus in teaching his disciples the model prayer. In those words so familiar to us, note that it does *not* say: "Forgive us our trespasses, just in case someday we might want to consider the remote possibility of forgiving those lousy so-and-sos who don't deserve it anyway." No, it says: "Forgive us our trespasses, *as* we forgive those who trespass against us." To the Ephesians: "Forgiving one another, *as* God in Christ has forgiven you." That one little word *as* says it all. If we are to ask for and accept God's forgiveness, we have no choice but to pass on to others this mysterious and precious gift. How on earth do we do this?

> *If we are to ask for and accept God's forgiveness, we have no choice but to pass on to others this mysterious and precious gift.*

ACCEPTING GOD'S FORGIVENESS

We begin by accepting the forgiveness that God gives us. This is not always as simple as it might seem. In order to accept fully the forgiveness that God offers, we need to believe that we are worthy of forgiveness. We live in a world in which we are valued for what we have, what we've done, and what others think about us. We are surrounded by voices telling us that we don't have enough, we haven't accomplished enough, we aren't smart enough, we aren't strong enough, we aren't attractive enough, we aren't popular enough; and we hear that little voice inside us telling us that we will *never* be good enough, no matter how hard we try. The truth is that, before anyone had a chance to judge us, God loved us. God's love for us does not depend on what we have, or what we've done, or what others think about us. God's love for us is absolute and constant.

Instead of worrying about who and where we are *not*, we need to accept that we are exactly who and where God wants us to be right now. In order to forgive and be forgiven, we must claim our identity in God. If our identity is in self, we are likely to listen to all the voices, including our own, that say we are not worthy of forgiveness, and to fear giving away too much of ourselves by forgiving those who try to take our self away and treat it as if it were worthless. In order to receive and offer reconciliation, we must claim a self whose very identity lies in God, a self we know can be neither given away nor stolen.

Accepting God's forgiveness also requires a willingness to let go of whatever is being forgiven. In his book *Dimensions of Prayer*, the great Quaker writer Douglas Steere speaks to this:

> There is . . . a condition for receiving God's gift of forgiveness. [We] must be willing to accept it. Absurd as this may seem, there are few who will believe in and accept the forgiveness of God so completely as to . . . leave their sin with [God] forever. They are always re-opening the vault where they have deposited their sin, . . . forever asking to have it back in order to fondle it, to reconstruct, to query, to worry over it . . . . Thus their sin ties them to the past.[2]

Throughout the liturgy of the Western church there appears many times the phrase "Lord, have mercy"—*Kyrie eleison*. The

Greek word *eleison*, which we translate "have mercy," means literally "to unbind." By asking for God's mercy, we are asking God to unbind us from those things past and present that separate us from God.

Forgiving God

As we look to those whom we must forgive, sometimes we need to begin by forgiving God. We may have grown up having a kind of codependent relationship with a vengeful, punishing God to whom we would not dare express anything critical, for fear of being slapped around or condemned to hell. We may actually carry a lot of repressed anger toward God. Even if our relationship is with a gentle, merciful God, anger is a natural and healthy part of such a relationship. There are times when we can feel betrayed by God, and we need to express those feelings honestly to God and listen for his response. The popular writer Madeleine L'Engle once wrote a letter to God that went like this:

> Dear God,
> I hate you.
> Love, Madeleine[3]

Sometimes we need not only to express our anger *to* God but also to direct our anger *at* God. Our dialogue with God about our anger can be an important part of our quest for reconciliation.

FORGIVING OUR SELF

The second person we must forgive is our self. To me this is the hardest part of forgiveness. I know intellectually that if God can forgive me, it is really presumptuous that I should be unable to forgive myself! But that's not where I am much of the time. My shame about who I am and my guilt about what I've done can be enormous barriers to my forgiveness of myself. Somehow I think that by controlling who I am now and what I do now, I can go back and pick up where I left off and make a different ending. I can't. No amount of will or effort will enable me to change who I have been or what I have done.

Forgiving myself means giving up hope for a better past.

Forgiving myself means giving up hope for a better past. In self-forgiveness I release the self of my past and claim the self of my present. There can be no reconciling love if there is no self to do the loving. In claiming my forgiven self I am once again free to love as God created me to love. By acknowledging the transforming power of God's grace in my life, I can now share the power of that grace with others.

FORGIVING OTHERS

Finally we come to forgiving those others. This is almost as hard as forgiving ourselves. I find that this is always much easier if I can consciously move from living in fear to living in love. The spiritual writer Marjorie Thompson (also the wife of John Mogabgab, whose words opened this chapter) lays the foundation for this important step:

> Forgiveness constitutes a decision to call forth and rebuild that love which is the only authentic ground of any human relationship. Such love forms the sole secure ground of our relationship with God as well. Indeed, it is only because God continually calls forth and rebuilds this love with us that we are capable of doing so with one another. Thus, to forgive is to participate in the mystery of God's love. [In the words of Alexander Pope:] "To err is human, to forgive divine." Genuine forgiveness draws us into the heart of divine life.[4]

To forgive others I must learn to accept them as imperfect creations of God, just as I must learn to accept myself as an imperfect creation of God. I know that I have hurt many people, often without being aware of how deeply I hurt them, or perhaps that I hurt them at all. Why do I assume that people who hurt *me* know exactly what they are doing and are doing it intentionally? When I can probe my past and identify so many factors that influence my current behavior, sometimes beyond my control, why do I assume that others are totally in control of *their* actions without the influences of *their* past?

To forgive is to participate in the mystery of God's love.
—Marjorie Thompson

When I can acknowledge my own brokenness, and sometimes even feel pity for my own woundedness, why is it so difficult for me to recognize the brokenness and woundedness of others? And why do I expect others to love me, when I find it so difficult to love them? They might be trying just as hard as I am and failing just as miserably. Forgiveness levels all of this on the solid ground of love. In the words of Henri Nouwen: "Forgiveness is the name of love practiced among people who love poorly." Accepting the woundedness of others allows us to feel *compassion*—which means literally "to suffer *with*." When my woundedness connects with the woundedness of another, then there is tolerance, acceptance, forgiveness, and healing for both of us.

> *Forgiveness is the name of love practiced among people who love poorly.*
>
> *—Henri Nouwen*

FORGIVING IS NOT FORGETTING

One of the great obstacles in our forgiveness of others is the misconception that to forgive means also to forget. We are afraid that to forgive someone is to say in effect: "It's all right. It doesn't really matter." And we can't bring ourselves to do that, certainly not if we were badly hurt by the other person's words or actions. Forgiving is not forgetting; indeed, if the offense was serious, we must *not* forget if we are to learn and grow from it. Abba Poemen, another of the Desert Fathers of fourth-century Egypt, said: "Not understanding what has happened prevents us from going on to something better." To forgive truly is to understand what happened, to claim the hurt, to face the wrong head-on, to name it, to count its cost, to say: "It is *not* all right, and it matters *very* deeply, but I forgive you." In this way God's grace flows through us, healing us as well as the person we are forgiving. We don't forget the offense; to forget would be to deny the value of the experience in our life. We let go of the bonds that trap us in continual replay of the event and all the pain that comes back with each remembrance.

The Parable of the Wicked Servant, which opens this chapter, is about us. Like all parables, it starts off being a story in which we see other people and ends up being a mirror in which we see ourselves. The first slave owed 10,000 talents—that was more than fifteen years' wages for a laborer in first-century Palestine. The second slave owed 100 denarii—exactly one hundred days' wages. So the first slave's debt was roughly five hundred times the debt of the second slave. How great is the debt that God has forgiven us? How does it compare to the debt that others owe us?

"Forgive us our trespasses, *as* we forgive those who trespass against us." "Forgiving one another, *as* God in Christ has forgiven you." It isn't that God forgives on an exchange basis. Our forgiveness of others is not a condition of God's forgiveness of us. Rather it is a condition of our *ability to receive* the forgiveness of God. If we are unable to open our heart to forgive another person, we will likewise be unable to open our heart to receive God's forgiveness of us. They are two sides of the same process.

Jesus said: "Blessed are the merciful, for they will receive mercy" (Matt 5:7). Mercy requires not only a right spirit on our part against a person who has wronged us, not only that we must overcome all vindictiveness, jealousy, and littleness, but also that we must do even more than feel a kind spirit in our heart. Jesus wept, but he did more than weep. He gave himself even unto death to serve and save those who had persecuted him.

Allan Knight Chalmers, in his book *High Wind at Noon*, tells the story of Peer Holm, who was a world-famous engineer. He built bridges, railroads, and tunnels in many parts of the world. He became wealthy and famous but later came to experience failure, sickness, and poverty. He returned to the small village where he was born and, together with his wife and little girl, eked out a meager living.

Peer Holm had a neighbor who owned a fierce dog. Peer warned him that the dog was dangerous, but the old man replied contemptuously, "Hold your tongue, you cursed pauper." One day Peer Holm came home to find the dog at the throat of his little girl. He tore the dog away, but the dog's teeth had gone too deeply, and the little girl was dead.

The sheriff shot the dog, and the neighbors were bitter against his owner. When sowing time came, they refused to sell him any grain. His plowed fields remained bare. Whenever he walked down the road, villagers sneered at him. But not Peer Holm. He could not sleep at night for thinking of his neighbor.

Early one morning he arose and got his last half bushel of barley. He climbed the fence and sowed seed in his neighbor's field. Soon, the fields revealed what he had done. When the young plants began to sprout, the field of the cruel neighbor became green, while part of Peer Holm's field remained bare.[5]

Mercy requires that we sow good seed in our enemy's field, even though it means that part of our own field will be left bare. It is not easy. It is the hardest possible action, but it opens us to the wholeness that God desires for each of us and allows God's forgiveness to flow through us, healing us and those to whom we pass it on.

FORGIVENESS AND GRACE

It has been said that justice is when we get what we deserve, mercy is when we don't get what we deserve, and grace is when we get what we don't deserve. The grace of God in our lives means that no matter who we are, where we have been, or what we have done, we will always have another chance. By accepting God's forgiveness and grace for ourselves, we accept also the responsibility to pass on that forgiveness and to reflect that grace to others. In doing so, we will free ourselves, heal our relationships, and find peace in God. "Blessed are the peacemakers, for they will be called children of God" (Matt 5:9). Peace is a gift from God, but it is not a gift to be jealously guarded. It is a gift to be shared for the reconciliation of the world.

The distinguished Swedish diplomat Dag Hammarskjöld, who served as the second Secretary General of the United Nations between 1953 and 1961, wrote in his diary:

> Forgiveness is the answer to the child's dream of a miracle by which what is broken is made whole again, what is soiled is made clean. The dream explains why we need to be forgiven, and why we must forgive. In the presence of God, nothing

stands between him and us—we are forgiven. But we cannot feel his presence if anything is allowed to stand between ourselves and others.[6]

No matter how much pain we may have suffered, surely none of us has experienced the agony and humiliation that Jesus experienced at his crucifixion. And yet, in the midst of all the excruciating pain and taunting ridicule, what did Jesus say? "Father, forgive them; for they know not what they do" (Luke 23:34a KJV). This is where the price was paid for each of us, and this is why we have no choice but to forgive as we have been forgiven.

So as we reach out to one another in love and our common brokenness, let us join hands at the foot of the cross and lift our eyes together to the figure that hangs above us, to see his pain and to hear his words once again: "Father, forgive them; for they know not what they do." And let us thank God for the answer, which comes to each of us: "I forgive you."

THIRTEEN

LOSING AND FINDING FAITH IN GOD

*I*mmediately *he made the disciples get into the boat and go on ahead to the other side, while he dismissed the crowds. And after he had dismissed the crowds, he went up the mountain by himself to pray. When evening came, he was there alone, but by this time the boat, battered by the waves, was far from the land, for the wind was against them. And early in the morning he came walking toward them on the sea. But when the disciples saw him walking on the sea, they were terrified, saying, "It is a ghost!" And they cried out in fear. But immediately Jesus spoke to them and said, "Take heart, it is I; do not be afraid." Peter answered him, "Lord, if it is you, command me to come to you on the water." He said, "Come." So Peter got out of the boat, started walking on the water, and came toward Jesus. But when he noticed the strong wind, he became frightened, and beginning to sink, he cried out, "Lord, save me!" Jesus immediately reached out his hand and caught him, saying to him, "You of little faith, why did you doubt?" When they got into the boat, the wind ceased. And those in the boat worshiped him, saying, "Truly you are the Son of God."*

—Matthew 14:22-33

Many of us lost through our active addiction any faith in God that we once had. Having consented to the miracle of recovery, how do we now nurture—or perhaps reconnect with—a faith in a Higher Power that will sustain us in our new life?

—∞— —∞— —∞—

The apostle Peter is an important figure in the Gospels. With Peter, what you see is what you get. He was a big, simple fisherman. He was rough, his skin weathered from countless hours in the blazing sun, his hands calloused from handling the nets of his trade. Peter was impulsive; he tended to leap before he looked: Ready, Fire, Aim!

For those of us in recovery, Peter reminds us of ourselves: eager to do the right thing but flawed and falling short. And yet, despite—or perhaps because of—his imperfections, God chose Peter for greatness.

The story of Jesus walking on the water was recorded in three of the four Gospels: Matthew, Mark, and John (cf. Mark 6:45-52; John 6:16-21). Of the three, however, only Matthew includes the story of Peter's attempt to walk on water. It is in this version of the story that we can see through Peter what it means to have faith in a Higher Power.

Jesus and his disciples had just finished feeding the five thousand on the shore of the Sea of Galilee. While he dismissed the crowds, Jesus made the disciples get into a boat and sent them on ahead to the opposite shore, a distance of about four and a half miles where they were at the northern end of the lake. Jesus then went up into the hills to pray. (The importance of being alone with God in deep prayer was illustrated by Jesus many times during his ministry.) By evening, the boat was far from shore—according to one account, more than halfway across the lake—and in the midst of a violent storm, buffeted by high winds, battered by heavy waves. Sometime between three and six in the morning, Jesus appeared, walking on the water. Now I imagine that would get the attention of most of us, even at that hour. The disciples were terrified and cried out, thinking they were seeing a ghost. Jesus spoke to them and said: "Take heart, it is I; do not be afraid."

This was a moment of divine revelation for Jesus' closest followers. Jesus not only identified himself as the miracle worker walking on the water; he used the same words that God had used many centuries earlier to identify himself to the Israelites, because the Greek text translated here "It is I" can also be translated "I AM." Here was Jesus, sounding like God, miraculously moving like God across the surface of the water to calm the storm and rescue the drowning—which, according to numerous references in the psalms, is what God does. In this unmistakably divine presence, Peter says: "Lord, if it is you, command me to come to you on the water." And Jesus says: "Come."

Haven't we all been in Peter's place? Haven't we all at some time said: "God, if it's really you, if this is really your will, give me a sign"? Peter said that. Jesus responded. And Peter stepped out of the boat.

At first everything was all right; in fact, it must have been pretty cool, walking on water like that. But soon Peter turned his attention away from Jesus to worry about the overwhelming force of the storm; and he began to sink. We do the same thing. We don't walk on water, but whenever we turn away from our Higher Power, the source of our strength, to focus on the source of our problems, we sink in other ways. Some of us drown.

Just like us, as he began to sink, Peter cried out: "Lord, save me!" How many times have we uttered that same cry? For Peter the terror did not last long. Immediately Jesus reached out his hand and caught him. "You of little faith," he said, "why did you doubt?"

It is tempting to infer from Jesus' rebuke that, if Peter had just

"Why did you doubt?"

had sufficient faith, he would have been able to walk on the water without sinking. If we were to apply that message to our own lives, we could attribute to lack of faith every accident, illness, and any other misfortune that causes us to sink. Chiding ourselves that, if we only had enough faith, we could overcome all our problems, we could spend the rest of our lives beating ourselves up over our lack of faith. Most of us don't need another reason to beat our self up. Jesus' question to Peter, "Why did you doubt?" was not about walking on water. Peter's problem began before he stepped out of the boat, demanding proof of the presence of Christ.

CALMING OUR STORM

This story is a powerful allegory for recovery. Entering sobriety, we can become so intently focused on our own program that we forget it's a "we" program. From the moment we enter sobriety, we never again have to be alone. We are surrounded by a worldwide community of people just like us; and we can reach out to any one of those persons, anywhere, at any hour of the day or night, and receive help. We never have to struggle alone. The members of this Fellowship are our fellow disciples in the boat of our recovery. At times we may be terrified by the storm raging around us, battering our boat. As with Peter, however, God in the person of Jesus comes to us in the boat of our life in recovery. Jesus didn't show up on the Sea of Galilee with his own lifeboat to rescue the drowning disciples. He walked calmly into *their* boat, just as he walks calmly into *our* boat, where we are being battered, and there he calms the storm. In another of Sister Macrina's poems, she writes about our life-storm:

> You begin your storm
>   under the Eye of God.
> A watchful, caring eye
>   gazes in your direction
>   as you wrestle
>   with the life force within.
>
> In the midst of these holy winds
> In the midst of this divine wrestling
>   your storm journey
>   like all hurricanes
>   leads you into the eye,
> Into the Eye of God
>   where all is calm and quiet.
>
> A stillness beyond imagining!
> Into the Eye of God
>   after the storm

Into the silent, beautiful darkness
Into the Eye of God.[1]

One night in Harlem in New York City, there was a terrible fire. In the building that was being consumed by flames, perched in a window on the fourth floor, was a little blind girl. The firefighters had become desperate. They couldn't fit the ladder truck between the buildings, and they were trying to get her to jump into the safety net, but she would not jump. She couldn't see the net, and she was scared. Finally her father arrived and shouted through a bullhorn that there was a net and that she was to jump on his command. The little girl jumped and was so completely relaxed that she did not break a single bone or strain a single muscle falling four stories. Because she trusted her father completely, she listened to his voice and did what he said was best. God holds a safety net under us at all times; if we listen to God's voice, no matter how far or how often we fall, God will always catch us, and we will always be safe.

BUT WHO DO YOU SAY THAT I AM?

Peter's journey of faith did not end that night on the water. As Jesus' ministry continued to unfold, Peter became a spokesman for the twelve apostles and a prototype of the Christian disciple; in fact, he has been called "Prince of the Apostles." One of the defining moments of his life came at Caesarea Philippi, where Jesus posed to the disciples a seminal question: "Who do people say that the Son of Man is?" And they said, "Some say John the Baptist, but others Elijah, and still others Jeremiah or one of the prophets." He said to them: "But who do you say that I am?" (Matt 16:13-15).

Not only is this question central to the Gospels; it is also essentially the question that each of us must answer in developing a personal relationship with our Higher Power, the God of our understanding.

Peter (who was originally named Simon) answered: "You are the Messiah, the Son of the living God." Jesus answered him, using first his birth name and then Jesus' new name for him: "Blessed are you, Simon son of Jonah! For flesh and blood has not revealed this to you, but my Father in heaven. And I tell you, you are Peter, and on this rock I will build my church. . . ." (Matt 16:16-18). Jesus' choice of Simon's new name was intentional: in Greek, Latin, Aramaic, and many modern languages, the name *Peter* means literally *rock*. (Some have suggested that's why he sank when he tried to walk on water.) So here we have Jesus proclaiming that Peter will be the rock upon which the Christian church will be founded—not bad for a humble fisherman "of little faith"!

Right up to the end, Peter tried to be faithful, but failed. On the night in which Jesus was betrayed and handed over to death, he prophesied to his disciples that they would all desert him. In Matthew's record of the exchange: "Peter said to him, 'Though all become deserters . . . I will never desert you.' Jesus said to him, 'Truly I tell you, this very night, before the cock crows, you will deny me three times.' Peter said to him, 'Even though I must die with you, I will not deny you' " (Matt 26:33-35). Later that same night, as Jesus was being tried before the high priests and council, Peter hung back in the outer courtyard; and, on three different occasions, he denied ever having known the innocent man inside who was being ridiculed, spat upon, and slapped. Peter had barely uttered his third denial when the cock crowed, and he remembered Jesus' words, and "he went out and wept bitterly" (Matt 26:75).

PEOPLE OF LITTLE FAITH

We live out Peter's story in our own lives. Like Peter, we are people of little faith. We want to follow the right path, and we go through the motions; but then the seas get rough, and we lose faith. We insist on stepping out of the boat, leaving our community of support, doubting, testing, blind to the many ways in which God reveals himself to us. We are quickly swept up in the storm of our problems, and we begin to sink. Before we can drown, God reaches out and rescues us. God comes into our boat and calms our storm. And, as with Peter, God looks into our eyes and says with sorrow in his voice: "Why did you doubt?"

As many times as we continue to test, we also continue to profess our faithfulness, until something unexpected happens, and we are called to stand up for our faith; and we shrink back in denial, just as Peter did. And yet God sees in us the potential for greatness, just as God saw Peter's potential for greatness.

Jesus chose Peter to be the head of the church. James and John asked for the chief places, but they were passed over, as were all the others. Peter was chosen because he sinned so shamefully but later wept so bitterly. He knew what it felt like to lose his faith and then find it again. He knew what it felt like to fall so far short that he landed in the sea of his own tears and then to feel the strong hand of God bearing him up once again. He knew what it felt like to repent and then to be surrounded by God's forgiveness

Like Peter, we are people of little faith.

and mercy. Peter sinned and repented; God forgave and loved him to greatness.

CHOOSING OUR ENDING

Like Peter, we are free to choose how our story ends. We will always come up short, just like Peter; we will never have enough faith, just like Peter; and, no matter how hard we try, we will continue, in our imperfection, to sin, just like Peter. But if we repent, as Peter did, then God will surround us with his forgiveness and mercy, just as he did Peter. And if we keep our eyes fixed on him, through all of life's storms, we will always be safe, and God—our Higher Power—will love us to greatness, just as he did Peter.

It doesn't take much. Jesus said to his disciples: "For truly I tell you, if you have faith the size of a mustard seed, you will say to this mountain, 'Move from here to there,' and it will move; and nothing will be impossible for you" (Matt 17:20b). Even if we start with only a little faith, through our Higher Power, nothing will be impossible for us either.

FOURTEEN

SAYING YES TO GOD

*I*n *the sixth month the angel Gabriel was sent by God to a town in Galilee called Nazareth, to a virgin engaged to a man whose name was Joseph, of the house of David. The virgin's name was Mary. And he came to her and said, "Greetings, favored one! The Lord is with you." But she was much perplexed by his words and pondered what sort of greeting this might be. The angel said to her, "Do not be afraid, Mary, for you have found favor with God. And now, you will conceive in your womb and bear a son, and you will name him Jesus. He will be great, and will be called the Son of the Most High, and the Lord God will give to him the throne of his ancestor David. He will reign over the house of Jacob forever, and of his kingdom there will be no end." Mary said to the angel, "How can this be, since I am a virgin?" The angel said to her, "The Holy Spirit will come upon you, and the power of the Most High will overshadow you; therefore the child to be born will be holy; he will be called Son of God. And now, your relative Elizabeth in her old age has also conceived a son; and this is the sixth month for her who was said to be barren. For nothing will be impossible with God." Then Mary said, "Here am I, the servant of the Lord; let it be with me according to your word." Then the angel departed from her.*

—Luke 1:26-38

In our quest to discover and embrace our own authentic image, the Program advises that we emulate others—"fake it till you make it." We may find a model in our sponsor or another member of a 12-Step group or perhaps a spiritual advisor. As discussed in chapter 7, we may subscribe to the WWJD (What Would Jesus Do?) approach. There is, however, one biblical character—often overlooked—who offers a perfect example of what it means to turn our will and our life over to the care of God as we understand God.

Most people, even non-Christians, understand that Mary was a major player in the Christmas story. She is represented in countless works of art depicting the Nativity, she is present in Nativity sets of all shapes and sizes, and she is remembered fondly in numerous carols of the season. Shortly after the holiday, however, throughout most of Protestant Christendom, Mary is packed up with Joseph, the baby, the shepherds, the wise men, the sheep, and the cows, and stored with the rest of the decorations, not to reappear until it's time to decorate for Christmas next year. This is regrettable, because Mary's significance for all Christians extends far beyond her role in the annual Christmas pageant. For those of us in recovery, she offers a powerful, year-round witness to the central theme in the Twelve Steps of Alcoholics Anonymous.

In the Christian tradition, Jesus is understood to be the Son of God, God in human form, God incarnate. As the mother of

Jesus, Mary is thus the Mother of God; Mother of the Church; Mother of the Messiah—the Redeemer—the one who paid the ultimate price for our salvation. She was also the first disciple of Jesus. She was the divine instrument chosen by God to bring into the world the Savior of the world. Hers was a singularly important and absolutely crucial role in the entire history of salvation.

We often hear the story of the Annunciation, where the angel tells Mary she will bear a child. As familiar as this story may be, have you ever stopped to consider how Mary felt? What did all of this look like from her perspective? It's easy for us to imagine Mary as a mature young woman who receives this strange message that she has this unusual task to perform before getting on with her life. It was not at all like that.

MARY'S REALITY

During Mary's lifetime, Middle Eastern society was almost totally dominated by men. Men virtually had all of the power, all of the rights, and made all of the important decisions. Most women were under the control of men all of their lives—first their father, and then, if they were fortunate, their husband. A male child could be expected to work and contribute to the family; by the time he was old enough to become a financial burden, he could generally earn at least as much as he cost the family. A girl, on the other hand, was a financial liability from the day of her birth—first from the cost of her upbringing and then from the cost of the dowry that would be required in order to marry her off so that she became someone else's responsibility. She had no opportunity for employment to offset her costs. Under Roman law (which was the law of the land), only the first female child had to be raised. All others could be "exposed," which meant legally abandoned, most likely to die, or to be taken by others to raise for domestic slavery or work in an inn or brothel. If food was scarce, boys got the greater portion, because they needed their strength to work. Girls were often malnourished well into adulthood. Following marriage in her early teens, the birth of a young woman's child was frequently fatal to the frail mother. Subsequent births posed similar health risks. It was not unusual for a young woman to marry into a family in which there were already children from a previous marriage in which the wife had died. This was very possibly Mary's situation. Scripture seems to indicate that Joseph was considerably older than she was, and the Gospels name several siblings of Jesus without any evidence that they were her children. These were the harsh realities of Mary's world. Mary could not possibly have imagined what God had planned for her, just as we cannot possibly imagine what God has planned for us.

We know almost nothing about Mary's background. She was a Jewish peasant girl, probably thirteen or fourteen years old when she was engaged to Joseph. In the society in which she lived, he was her best hope for a decent life. According to ancient Jewish custom, the marriage was sealed with the engagement. The bride-to-be would live at home for a year following the engagement, at the end of which the groom would come to take her to his home, where the wedding would take place. Even if the angel had not appeared, Mary's future was frighteningly uncertain. With her engagement she had been legally severed from her family of origin. The quality of her life was now largely dependent upon the kind of husband Joseph turned out to be and how his relatives accepted and treated her. Once the angel showed up, however, all bets were off.

Joseph's Reality

Scripture tells us that Mary was still a virgin. Becoming pregnant before the marriage was consummated would be attributed to adultery and would have disastrous consequences. Under Jewish law, her husband-to-be, Joseph, had two choices: he could take her to court and expose her publicly, in which case the punishment prescribed by law was death by stoning; or he could give her a writ of divorce and send her away, in which case she would never be able to remarry under Hebrew law. According to Matthew's Gospel (1:19), he opted for the latter: "Joseph, being a righteous man and unwilling to expose her to public disgrace, planned to dismiss her quietly." Either way, Mary would lose any hope of a decent life. This is what she faced in receiving the angel's message.

Put yourself in Mary's place. What would you have said? Can you even imagine how you would feel? To Mary it must have felt like "hitting bottom." No matter how unpleasant her life could have been, she knew generally what to expect; the role was familiar, predictable, reasonably secure. What the angel Gabriel proposed had never before happened in the history of humankind. The role that he described for her was totally new, utterly unfamiliar, and undoubtedly terrifying. And yet, face to face with this incomprehensible miracle and its potentially devastating consequences, how did this young girl respond?

She did not say: "I can't possibly do this" or "God, don't mess up my life like this" or even "Why me?" She said: "Here am I, the servant of the Lord; let it be with me according to your word." In the words her Son would utter many years later: "not my will but yours be done" (Luke 22:42b).

OUR REALITY

Was there an angel, or angels, in your life who brought you the message that you had been chosen by God to participate in the miracle of recovery? How did you greet the prospect of that miracle? As painful and unmanageable as your life may have become, could you even imagine going through the rest of your life without taking a drink or drug or engaging in whatever destructive behavior brought you to recovery? I couldn't. I was, as the Big Book says, "unable to imagine life either with alcohol or without it."[1] Alcohol had been my daily companion for more than thirty years. How could I possibly live without it?

Two thousand years ago, Mary understood what we in Alcoholics Anonymous must also understand, if we are to "become happily and usefully whole": unless we let go of our self-centeredness, our self-will, and our fear, our lives will remain unmanageable, and we will remain "restless, irritable, and discontented." Like every one of us, Mary "stood at the turning point"— and what a turning point it was! With complete abandon she turned her will and her life over to the care of God, as she understood God. She "let go and let God," and God worked in her life a miracle beyond any human comprehension.

Like Mary, we are called to let go of a way of life that is familiar, comfortable, predictable and to let God lead us into a life that is unknown, challenging, even frightening. Mary could not possibly imagine what God had planned for her, just as we cannot possibly imagine what God

If we "let go and let God," we will be blessed beyond anything we can imagine.

has planned for us. What was true for Mary, however, is every bit as true for us: If we "let go and let God," we will be blessed beyond anything we can imagine; God will use us to be a blessing to God's world; and we will find what the apostle Paul called "the peace of God, which surpasses all understanding" (Phil 4:7). We will become, in the language of AA, "happy, joyous, and free."

There is no more perfect example of what it means to say yes to God's plan for our life than the life and yes of Mary. No matter how insurmountable the difficulties or how overwhelming the future may seem, we will forever share with Mary the assurance of the angel Gabriel: "For nothing is impossible with God." We can expect nothing less from our Higher Power. With that assurance and the strength we receive from our Higher Power, we can affirm and participate fully in God's plan for our life.

Here am I, the servant of the Lord; let it be with me according to your word.

FIFTEEN

SURRENDER TO LIVE

A fter these things God tested Abraham. He said to him, "Abraham!" And he said, "Here I am." He said, "Take your son, your only son Isaac, whom you love, and go to the land of Moriah, and offer him there as a burnt offering on one of the mountains that I shall show you." So Abraham rose early in the morning, saddled his donkey, and took two of his young men with him, and his son Isaac; he cut the wood for the burnt offering, and set out and went to the place in the distance that God had shown him. On the third day Abraham looked up and saw the place far away. Then Abraham said to his young men, "Stay here with the donkey; the boy and I will go over there; we will worship, and then we will come back to you." Abraham took the wood of the burnt offering and laid it on his son Isaac, and he himself carried the fire and the knife. So the two of them walked on together. Isaac said to his father Abraham, "Father!" And he said, "Here I am, my son." He said, "The fire and the wood are here, but where is the lamb for a burnt offering?" Abraham said, "God himself will provide the lamb for a burnt offering, my son." So the two of them walked on together. When they came to the place that God had shown him, Abraham built an altar there and laid the wood in order. He bound his son Isaac, and laid him on the altar, on top of the wood. Then Abraham reached out his *hand and took the knife to kill his son. But the angel of the LORD called to him from heaven, and said, "Abraham, Abraham!" And he said, "Here I am." He said, "Do not lay your hand on the boy or do anything to him; for now I know that you fear God, since you have not withheld your son, your only son, from me." And Abraham looked up and saw a ram, caught in a thicket by its horns. Abraham went and took the ram and offered it up as a burnt offering instead of his son. So Abraham called that place "The LORD will provide"; as it is said to this day, "On the mount of the LORD it shall be provided." The angel of the LORD called to Abraham a second time from heaven, and said, "By myself I have sworn, says the LORD: Because you have done this, and have not withheld your son, your only son, I will indeed bless you, and I will make your offspring as numerous as the stars of heaven and as the sand that is on the seashore. And your offspring shall possess the gate of their enemies, and by your off-spring shall all the nations of the earth gain blessing for them-selves, because you have obeyed my voice." So Abraham returned to his young men, and they arose and went together to Beer-sheba; and Abraham lived at Beer-sheba.*

—Genesis 22:1-19

The first three Steps bring us to a point of surrender without which the remaining nine Steps are not possible. This chapter is about that "turning point" beyond which the miracle of recovery unfolds, the point at which we receive what one story in the Big Book (4th ed.) calls "the Keys of the Kingdom."

We are special. Those of us who have been afflicted with addiction are very special people. We have what since 1956 has been recognized by the American Medical Association as an illness, and we make up only about 10 percent of the general population. We are indeed special.

And yet, in what I believe is the single most important—and most difficult—aspect of our recovery, we are not at all special; in fact, we are exactly like every other human being who has ever lived. We all share an inherent belief, reinforced at every turn by our culture, that, in order to be truly happy, we must get more money than we have gotten, have more possessions than we have, look better than we look, be smarter than we are, have more power than we have, command more respect than we command, and, above all, we must take control of our lives if we are ever even to hope to achieve these elusive goals. On this treadmill of existence, happiness is always out of reach, and we live—and eventually die—in a state of constant, miserable frustration. We live in a cult of self, in which we bury our spiritual essence under our human compulsiveness—exacerbated by our addictions—and we remain perpetually "restless, irritable, and discontented."

The Big Book diagnoses this problem: "Selfishness—self-centeredness! That, we think, is the root of our troubles."[1] Later the book describes the alcoholic as "an extreme example of self-will run riot"[2] and asserts that "any life run on self-will can hardly be a success."[3] The introductory material in the chapter "How It Works" states: "Some of us tried to hold on to our old ideas and the result was nil until we let go absolutely."[4] The Third Step Prayer asks: "Relieve me from the bondage of self."[5]

This is not a new problem, and it is not in the least restricted to alcoholics and drug addicts. As introduced in chapter 7, the problem originated in the Garden of Eden. Instead of listening to God, we chose to listen to a serpent, which told us that we cannot trust God to provide for us. If we want to be truly happy, we must take control of our own lives and get for ourselves what we cannot trust

> *Some of us tried to hold on to our old ideas and the result was nil until we let go absolutely.*
> *—Big Book*

God to give us. And we lost the paradise in which God intended for us to live. That serpent still speaks to us today, and we still listen.

There is a story of an Irishman who was driving down the street in a panic, because he had an important meeting and couldn't find a parking place. Looking up to heaven he said: "Lord, take pity on me. If you find me a parking place, I will go to Mass every Sunday for the rest of me life and give up me Irish whiskey." Miraculously, a parking place appeared. He looked up again and said: "Never mind, I found one." We enact our own versions of that story every day.

SURRENDER TO WIN

In Twelve-Step Programs of recovery, we express it very simply: "Surrender to win." It's a familiar and important slogan for early recovery. It is the essence of the first three Steps:

- **Step One**—admitting that my life is completely unmanageable by me, and that I need to surrender my grasping control of it.
- **Step Two**—coming to believe that there is One to whom I can surrender control, One who can take whatever is left of me and restore me to a condition of wholeness.
- **Step Three**—making a decision to surrender my will and my life to the care of One who loves me more than I will ever be able to comprehend, One who wants only the best for me, and One who has the power to make all things work together for good in my life.

These first three Steps are sometimes summarized: "I can't, He can, I think I'll let Him." Veterans of the Program say: "The Program works when I let it work." If we don't let it work, it will never work. We have to allow God to do for us what we cannot do for ourselves. No matter how hard we try, we cannot work miracles. Only God can work miracles and only if we let him. Each of us who has made it into recovery is a living witness to that reality. And to those ready to join us in this journey, we offer a "surrender chip" as a token of encouragement and commitment. "Let go and let God," "surrender to win."

The Program works when I let it work.
—Veterans of the Program

OFFERING UP OUR SELF

The word *surrender* comes from the French phrase *se rendre*, which means "to offer up oneself." The process of surrender is a process of offering up ourselves to God. It is this "offering up" that is at the heart of Jesus' call to discipleship: "If any want to become my followers, let them deny themselves and take up their cross daily and follow me. For those who want to save their life will lose it, and those who lose their life for my sake will save it" (Luke 9:23, 24). The message is clear: we must die to self in order to be alive to God.

The twentieth-century German theologian Dietrich Bonhoeffer described the process: "To deny oneself is to be aware only of Christ and no more of self. . . . Only when we have become completely oblivious to self are we ready to bear the cross for Christ's sake."[6] The Nobel physicist Albert Einstein once wrote: "The true value of a human being is determined primarily by the measure and the sense in which he has attained liberation from the self."[7] C. S. Lewis described what he called "the infinite relief of having for once got rid of all the silly nonsense about your own dignity which has made you restless and unhappy all your life."[8]

> *What is most important is our willingness to surrender, to offer ourselves up to the care of a Power greater than ourselves.*

In Alcoholics Anonymous, we express it simply as our Third Step, in which we "made a decision to turn our will and our life over to the care of God as we understand him." The depth of our understanding of God is not important. What is most important is our willingness to surrender, to offer ourselves up to the care of a Power greater than ourselves. In doing so, we cease being our own god, we cease making other things into gods, and we abandon all other sources of security in favor of the One God who loves us and sets us free. We cease living in fear and begin living in love.

In one of her meditations for the recovery community, Karen Casey writes:

> Being overly preoccupied with ourselves stunts our spiritual growth, just as it limits all we do. We cannot realize our full potential when we are concentrating on our desires or fears. We cannot hear the voice of our Inner Guide when we are listening to the voice of our anxiety. Our recovery can be measured by our progress in getting out of ourselves.
>
> That's why we are asked to turn our will and our life over to the care of God. The relinquishment of self to a Higher Power is the key to personal freedom. Our addictions are only symptoms of our underlying disease—the disease of self-centeredness. Surrendering the self automatically puts us in touch with the power of the universe—our Creator.[9]

COCREATOR WITH GOD

When we stop being ruled by our own fear-driven agendas, goals, and devices, and we begin to listen for God's guidance, we enter a partnership with God. We become a cocreator with God. The popular author Max Lucado recalls his own discovery of this collaboration:

It's a wonderful day indeed when we stop working for God and begin working with God. . . . For years I viewed God as a compassionate CEO and my role as a loyal sales representative. He had his office, and I had my territory. I could contact him as much as I wanted. He was always a phone call or fax away. He encouraged me, rallied behind me, and supported me, but he didn't go with me. At least I didn't think he did. Then I read 2 Corinthians 6:1: We are "God's fellow workers" (NIV).

Fellow workers? Co-laborers? God and I together? Imagine the paradigm shift this truth creates. Rather than report to God, we work with God. Rather than check in with him and then leave, we check in with him and then follow. We are always in the presence of God. There is never a nonsacred moment. His presence never diminishes. Our awareness of his presence may falter, but the reality of his presence never changes.[10]

The most marvelous wisdom on surrender that I know may be found in a book entitled *Abandonment to Divine Providence*, which is a collection of teachings by an eighteenth-century French Jesuit named Jean-Pierre de Caussade. Here is a sampling of Caussade's wisdom, with notations in square brackets relating each teaching to the Steps and Principles of 12-Step recovery:

- God reveals himself to the humble in the lowliest of disguises, but the proud, who never look below the surface, fail to find him even in his greatest manifestations. [Steps Six and Seven; humility]
- In reality, holiness consists of one thing only: complete loyalty to God's will. . . . It is the ready acceptance of all that

comes to us at each moment of our lives. [Step Eleven; acceptance]

- We have to do nothing except allow his holy will to work within us and surrender ourselves to it blindly with absolute confidence. [Steps Three and Eleven; faith, trust]

- God's action is boundless in its scope and power, but it can only fill our souls if we empty them of all false confidence in our own ability. [Steps Three, Six, and Seven; faith, humility]

- We cannot enjoy true peace unless we submit to God's will. [Steps Three and Eleven; faith, trust]

- Do you for one moment imagine you will find peace by resisting the Almighty? It is rather this resistance, which we often keep up without realizing it, that is the source of all our trouble. [Step Three; surrender]

- To be satisfied with the present moment is to relish and adore the divine will moving through all we have to do and suffer as events crowd in upon us. [Step Three; acceptance, spiritual awareness]

- Now let me tell you that the will of God is all that is necessary, and what it does not give you is of no use to you at all. [Steps Three and Eleven; faith, trust]

- You have nothing to do but love and cherish what each moment brings, considering it as the best possible thing for you and having perfect confidence in God's activities, which cannot do anything but good. [Step Three; faith, trust]

- Now it is surely obvious that the only way to receive the impress of this idea is to put oneself quietly in the hands of God and that none of our own efforts and mental striving can be of any use at all. This work in our souls cannot be accomplished by cleverness, intelligence, or any subtlety of mind, but only by completely abandoning ourselves to the divine action, becoming like metal poured into a mold, or a canvas waiting for the brush, or marble under the sculptor's hands. It is surely clear that we shall not assume that image which the eternal wisdom wishes us to have by trying to understand all the mysterious activities of God down through the centuries. We can receive God's seal on our soul only by abandoning our will to him, not by any efforts of our reason. [Step Three; surrender, faith, trust]

- This state of abandonment is a blending of faith, hope, and love in one single act which unites us to God and all his activities. When these three virtues are united, they, of course, become one and so form a single act, a single raising of the heart to God and a simple abandonment to him. [Step Three; surrender]

- The essence of spirituality is contained in this phrase: "complete and utter abandonment to the will of God." [Steps Three and Eleven; surrender, faith, trust]

- When God becomes our guide, he insists that we trust him without reservations and put aside all nervousness about his guidance. [Step Three; surrender, faith, trust]

- There is nothing safer and less likely to lead us astray than the darkness of faith. [Step Three; faith, trust]

- At every moment God's will produces what is needful for the task in hand, and the simple soul, instructed by faith, finds everything as it should be and wants neither more nor less than what it has. [Steps Three and Eleven; faith, trust, acceptance]

- The realization that God is active in all that happens at every moment is the deepest knowledge we can have in this life of the things of God. [Steps Three and Eleven; faith, trust, spiritual awareness][11]

The marvelous, timeless wisdom that Caussade teaches is the heart of spirituality, and spirituality is the heart of our recovery.

The psalmist wrote: "Be still, and know that I am God!" (Ps 46:10). The Hebrew verb commonly translated "be still" does not mean "stop talking"—or as we say in the South, "hush." It means "relax." The sense is that of hold- ing something from above at arm's

Let go and know that I am God.

length and opening your hand to let it drop. In the Program we call it "letting go." For us the psalm could read: "Let go and know that I am God." There is no better summary of God's instructions for our recovery: "Let go and know that I am God."

WHY IS THIS SO DIFFICULT?

Why do we have such trouble letting go? What on earth are we clinging to? Who among us has a track record of managing his or her life that is so stellar that we can't imagine that God could possibly improve on it? None of us got here on a winning streak. I don't know anyone whose life was going so well that he or she woke up one morning and said: "I think I'll check myself into a treatment center just to see if this could possibly get any better." And as much as we may have tried to blame our misery on others, it was never about them. We hit bottom when we—and *only we*—had done such a thorough job of destroying our life and the lives of those closest to us that we had nowhere else to turn. What on earth are we clinging to?

We're clinging to our human nature. We're clinging to the very weakest part of us, the part that *we* created—our false self, our self-centered ego—instead of the part of us that *God* created—our spiritual nature, our divine core, lovingly crafted by God in God's own image and likeness. In our divine core, underneath all the hardness of our false self, where we are still soft and still bear the fingerprints of the Divine Potter who shaped us, our heart and the heart of God are one. How long has it been since you were in touch with that soft core? Why do we cling to our human nature when the essence of life is in our spiritual nature?

We cling to our human nature because we are also victims of our own short-sightedness. Our reactions to life events are always based on our limited vision and our even more limited understanding, which accounts for our limited success. God has no limitations.

There is a Chinese story of an old farmer who had an old horse for tilling his fields. One day the horse escaped into the hills. When all of the farmer's neighbors sympathized with the old man

176

over his bad luck, the farmer replied: "Bad luck? Good luck? Who knows?" A week later the horse returned with a herd of wild horses from the hills, and this time the neighbors congratulated the farmer on his good luck. His reply was: "Good luck? Bad luck? Who knows?" Then, when the farmer's son was attempting to tame one of the wild horses, he fell off its back and broke his leg. Everyone thought this very bad luck. Not the farmer, whose only reaction was: "Bad luck? Good luck? Who knows?" Some weeks later, the army marched into the village and conscripted every able-bodied youth they found there. When they saw the farmer's son with his broken leg, they let him off. "Good luck? Bad luck? Who knows?" And that is precisely the point. We cannot possibly know what God can do with the events of our life, unless we let him.

Obedience and Faith

In the story of Abraham and Isaac, we find a deep and troubling obedience. In utter trust in God and utter dependence on God's provision, Abraham comes to the point of sacrificing the one who is most dear to him. Here is letting go indeed! Abraham allows neither doubt nor affection to stand between himself and the will of God. The reason can only be that he *knows* God, and so is infinitely confident of what God will do. What is central is that Abraham *responds to the Word of God.* Hearing a promise, a threat, a commandment, he acts accordingly. He does not cling to his own natural interests or assumptions about himself, to his own dignity or his own infirmity, or even to his own love for

Isaac. None of these things becomes an idol for him. He becomes a model of simplicity and abandonment, of letting go. No part of his life is held back from the service of God; there is nothing that he will not believe or do or sacrifice when God speaks. This ready self-abandonment is at the heart of his faith.

When Abraham heard a word from God, he did not look for ways to defend himself against it. Rather than trying to preserve the status quo or maintain his own standing, Abraham accepted God as God. The self-abandonment that is the heart of Christian spirituality requires a total trust in God, a total willingness for God to be God. The longer we remain in the Word of God, the more deeply we know the truth, the all-encompassing reality that is God. Knowing this reality sets us free for trust. Faith gives us access to the reality of God; living with this reality deepens our faith into absolute reliance. Each idol we are able to let go of is one less curtain veiling God from our sight. As we become more transparent to the presence of God, each moment spent in that presence brings a greater readiness to let go of anything that is not God. Those who rely solely and utterly on God do as Abraham did; they know the truth, and the truth sets them free.

Put yourself in Abraham's place. Can you imagine what it

> *The self-abandonment that is the heart of Christian spirituality requires a total trust in God, a total willingness for God to be God.*

would feel like to be called upon by God to kill your only child? Would you respond as Abraham did: "Here I am, Lord"; or would your response be more like: "What!? You must be kidding!" Faced with what appeared to be a horrible prospect, Abraham did not seize control of the situation and go his own way, assuming he knew better than God what was best for him and his family. He responded in faith, and God not only spared his son, but also established with Abraham a covenant that became a blessing to the whole world.

Do you think Abraham had any idea that things would turn out as they did? Do you think that Mary, kneeling at the foot of the cross, holding in her arms the broken body of her dead son, covered in blood and sweat and dirt and spit, could possibly have known how that would turn out? The astounding reality is that our God is a God who can turn an unwanted teenage pregnancy into the birth of the Messiah. Our God is a God who can turn a brutal crucifixion into a miraculous resurrection that brings salvation to the world. Our God is a God who can turn a hopeless life destroyed by addiction into an exciting journey filled with joy. Why do we insist on working against our God by exercising our own will instead of opening ourselves to God's will for our lives?

A man attending the cinema in New York became increasingly irritated by the person behind him, who kept asking his companion: "What happened?" "What's going on?" The man thought, *It's not that hard a film to follow!* To make matters worse, the person's knee or foot or something kept thump-thump-thumping the back of his seat. To send the offending person a message, the man cast several annoyed glances over his shoulder, but to no effect. As he was wondering what to say to the jerk, he suddenly felt someone licking his ear. That was the last straw. Whirling around, he found himself face-to-face with a German shepherd guide dog. He did a double take, after which the dog licked his face, repeatedly. "Aw," he whispered, reaching around to scratch the dog's head. "What a good dog." The owner groped for the dog's harness, coaxed the animal back to the floor, and the man returned to the movie, feeling guilty but no longer minding the thump-thump-thumping of what he now knew to be the dog's tail on the back of his seat.

Things are often not what they seem. The woman who cut us off in traffic last night could be a single mother who had worked nine hours that day and was rushing home to cook dinner, help with homework, do the laundry, and spend a few precious moments with her children. That pierced, tattooed, disinterested young man who couldn't make correct change at the supermarket checkout could be a nineteen-year-old college student balancing his apprehension over final exams with his fear of not getting his student loans for next semester. That scary-looking bum begging for money in the same spot every day could be an alcoholic/addict—one of us—who hasn't been able to find his way to recovery. That old couple walking so annoyingly slowly through the store aisles and blocking our shopping progress could be savoring this moment, knowing that, according to the biopsy report she got back last week, this will be the last year that they go shopping together.

We simply can't see far enough or understand enough to take

control. That's why we trust God, who sees and understands everything. In the ancient wisdom found in the book of Proverbs: "Trust in the LORD with all your heart, and do not rely on your own insight. In all your ways acknowledge him, and he will make straight your paths" (Prov 3:5, 6).

Learning to trust God often involves overcoming our own bad habits. The eighteenth-century British literary figure Samuel Johnson once wrote: "The chains of habit are too weak to be felt until they are too strong to be broken." In recovery, we work to break our bad habits by practicing good habits. We surrender old behaviors while we condition new behaviors. We surrender *our* will in favor of God's will, and we do it daily, if we want to stay clean and sober.

Continuous, uninterrupted surrender followed by continuous, uninterrupted action.

A friend of mine in the Program characterizes his life in recovery as "continuous, uninterrupted surrender followed by continuous, uninterrupted action." Not only is that a great recipe for recovery; it is also precisely how the Twelve Steps are organized. Steps One through Three lead to surrender, without which recovery is not possible. Steps Four through Twelve lead to action, which determines the quality of our recovery.

A SIMPLE PROGRAM

I begin every day exactly like every other alcoholic: I wake up with untreated alcoholism. How I treat my disease that day will determine whether I stay sober, but I have to do it for only one day. At Cumberland Heights, the treatment center where I got sober and with which I have been affiliated since my release, we advise patients that there are five things we must do every day in order to stay clean and sober—and every one of them involves surrender, getting us out of self:

1. Start the day on our knees, thanking God for the gift of a new day and the miracle of waking up instead of regaining consciousness, and asking God to remove from us, for just that one day, the desire for drink or drug

2. Read something from the literature (AA literature, spiritual literature, preferably both)

3. Talk to another alcoholic/addict, preferably our sponsor

4. Go to a meeting

5. End the day on our knees, thanking God for keeping us clean and sober that day

I have never heard of anyone who has heard of anyone who relapsed on a day when that person did all five of those things. In a life in which there are no guarantees, that may be the closest thing to a guarantee we will ever get, and we receive it anew every day, one day at a time. It couldn't be much simpler.

No matter how simple it is, however, or how well we understand it, we will never do it perfectly. We will never be able to let go absolutely for all time. We are imperfect creatures, and we will always act imperfectly. Working a program of recovery is not about achieving sobriety. After about three days, we won't get any more sober. Working a program of recovery is about the *quality* of our sobriety.

The rewards come not in achieving perfection, but rather in striving always for improvement. It's a process, not an event. In the words of the Big Book: "We claim spiritual progress rather than spiritual perfection."[12] Practice doesn't make perfect; practice makes better. As an assertion attributed to Mother Teresa reminded us: "God does not call us to be successful; God calls us to be faithful." It is our faithful trying that most pleases God, not our final attainment of perfection. God already has all the perfection he needs; he doesn't need us to add to it. What God wants is our brokenness, freely given, with no self-will attached. The

> *God does not ask our ability or our inability; God asks only our availability.*

psalmist wrote: "The sacrifice acceptable to God is a broken spirit; a broken and contrite heart, O God, you will not despise" (Ps 51:17). Martin Luther is purported to have written: "God creates out of nothing; therefore, until a man is nothing, God can make nothing out of him." God wants our brokenness, and our willingness to live in total surrender. God does not ask our ability or our inability; God asks only our availability.

In a collection of writings entitled *Thoughts in Solitude*, the twentieth-century Trappist monk Thomas Merton wrote:

> My Lord God, I have no idea where I am going. I do not see
> the road ahead of me. I cannot know for certain where it will

end. Nor do I really know myself, and the fact that I think I am following your will does not mean that I am actually doing so.

But I believe the desire to please you does in fact please you. And I hope that I have that desire in all that I am doing. I hope that I will never do anything apart from that desire. And I know that if I do this, you will lead me by the right road, though I may know nothing about it. Therefore I will trust you always though I may seem to be lost and in the shadow of death. I will not fear, for you are ever with me, and you will never leave me to face my perils alone.[13]

One of the many valuable lessons I learned in early recovery was this: "Life is hard, but it does not have to be a struggle." After many years of numbness, when I could finally feel again and could tell when I was struggling, I discovered that the cause of my struggling was invariably the same: there was too much *me* in the equation. When I got myself out of the equation, I stopped struggling, everything relaxed, and things worked the way God intended.

Surrender involves giving up something that not only doesn't work, but will never work, in favor of something that not only does work, but will always work.

Jesus said: "Truly I tell you, unless you change and become like children, you will never enter the kingdom of heaven" (Matt 18:3). Here sobriety and the kingdom of heaven intersect.

A child is innocent, open, accepting, trusting, vulnerable, eager to share, ready to love. This is what surrender looks like; this is what spiritual maturity looks like; this is what reliance on a Higher Power looks like; and this is what we must feel like, if we are to enter fully both the world of recovery and the kingdom of heaven. Surrender involves giving up something that not only doesn't work, but will *never* work, in favor of something that not only does work, but will *always* work.

Surrender to win—by all means! But if we really want to live, if we really want to savor all of the freedom and hope and joy that recovery offers, if we really want to keep winning, we must keep surrendering—every day, every hour, every minute, if necessary. Because life in self is no life at all. Life in God is beyond anything we can even dream. Surrender to live!

A Prayer for Faith

Gracious and loving God, as we turn our wills and our lives over to you, help us to let go absolutely. You have raised us out of the miry pit, out of the mud and clay, and set our feet upon the solid path; and yet we are too often anxious about where that path will lead us. Grant us the faith we need to follow the path that you have set before us. When we walk to the edge of all the light we have and prepare to take that first step into the darkness of the unknown, help us know that, by your grace, either there will be something solid for us to stand on, or we will be taught to fly. As much as we might prefer an easier, softer way, you call us to leap, in faith, as a trusting child leaps into the arms of a loving parent. As we take that leap, may we know in our hearts, as surely as that child knows, that we will be totally safe, because we are too precious to let fall. Amen.

NOTES

Preface

1. Anonymous, *Alcoholics Anonymous*, 4th ed. (New York: Alcoholics Anonymous World Services, 2002) [hereinafter Big Book], 44.
2. Macrina Wiederkehr, *A Tree Full of Angels: Seeing the Holy in the Ordinary* (New York: HarperCollins, 1988).
3. Anonymous, *'Pass It On': The Story of Bill Wilson and How the A.A. Message Reached the World* (New York: Alcoholics Anonymous World Services, 1984), 147.

1. Do You Want to Be Made Well?

1. Big Book, 568.
2. Ibid., 58.
3. Ernest Kurtz and Katherine Ketcham, *The Spirituality of Imperfection: Storytelling and the Journey to Wholeness* (New York: Bantam Books, 1992), 168.

2. Finding Our Way out of the Darkness

1. Dr. Claypool chronicled his journey through the grief caused by his daughter's death in *Tracks of a Fellow Struggler*, rev. ed. (New Orleans: Insight Press, 1995).
2. C. S. Lewis, *A Grief Observed* (New York: Bantam Books, 1976), 4-5.
3. Henri J. M. Nouwen, *Turn My Mourning into Dancing* (Nashville: Thomas Nelson, 2001), 16.
4. The Nietzsche quotation is from his essay *Twilight of the Idols* (1889); Dr. King's thoughts appear in David Garrow, *Bearing the Cross: Martin Luther King, Jr., and the Southern Christian Leadership Conference* (New York: HarperCollins, 2004), 532, and many other sources.
5. Big Book, 14.
6. Anonymous, *Twelve Steps and Twelve Traditions* (New York: Alcoholics Anonymous World Services, 1981) [hereafter 12 X 12], 46.
7. Ibid., 49.
8. Ibid., 97.
9. Ibid., 110.

3. Choose Life

1. Big Book, 53.
2. Research summarized in Laurie Buchanan, "Healthy Boundaries," *The Monthly Aspectarian* (November 2009), online version at www.lightworks.com.
3. Big Book, 83.
4. Ibid., 62.
5. Charles Allen, *All Things Are Possible Through Prayer* (Grand Rapids, MI: F. H. Revell Co., 1958), 28-29.

4. Beginning Again

1. Personal communication from Victor Fried. Used by permission.
2. Big Book, 83.
3. Elie Wiesel, *Messages of God: Biblical Portraits and Legends* (New York: Random House, 1976), 32.
4. Big Book, 133.

6. You Are Called by Name

1. Wiederkehr, *Angels* (see preface, note 2), 11.
2. Ibid., 14.

7. Claiming Our Authentic Self

1. The traditional translation in the Psalter of Miles Coverdale (1535) cited here is particularly poignant.

8. Standing on Holy Ground

1. Radio broadcast from 1981.
2. Craig Brian Larson, *750 Engaging Illustrations for Preachers, Teachers, and Writers* (Grand Rapids, MI: Baker Books, 2007), 345.
3. John Mogabgab, "Editor's Introduction," *Weavings: A Journal of the Christian Spiritual Life* 7, no. 5 (September–October 1992): 2.
4. Macrina Wiederkehr, *Seasons of Your Heart: Prayers and Reflections*, rev. ed. (New York: HarperCollins, 1991), 4.

9. Living into Our Importance

1. William Robbins, "Kansas City Journal; Acts of Charity Spring from Rock of Honesty," *The New York Times* (December 16, 1990),

http://www.nytimes.com/1990/12/16/us/kansas-city-journal-acts-of-charity-spring-from-rock-of-honesty.html.

2. Wiederkehr, *Angels*, 95-96.

10. Learning to Pray

1. C. S. Lewis, *Surprised by Joy* (New York: Harcourt Brace Jovanovich, 1955), 227, also *Christian Reflections* (Grand Rapids, MI: William B. Eerdmans Publishing Company, 1967), 169.

2. Abraham J. Twerski, *Living Each Day* (Brooklyn, NY: Artscroll Mesorah Publications, 1988), 70.

3. Søren Kierkegaard, *Christian Discourses*, trans. Walter Lowrie (Oxford: Oxford University Press, 1940), 324.

4. Kieran Kavanaugh, ed. and trans., *The Collected Works of St. John of the Cross* (Washington: ICS Publications, 1991), 92; the context is the Prologue to the Fourth Gospel, see John 1:1-18.

5. Thomas Keating, *Invitation to Love* (New York: Continuum, 2001), 90.

6. Eugene H. Peterson, *Subversive Spirituality* (Grand Rapids, MI: Wm. B. Eerdmans Publishing Company, 1997), 237.

7. Thomas Merton in *Dublin Review* 223 (1949): 28; quoted in M. Basil Pennington, *Thomas Merton, Brother Monk: The Quest for True Freedom* (San Francisco: Harper & Row, 1987), 160; also in Kenneth Leech, *Soul Friend*, rev. ed. (Harrisburg, PA: Morehouse Publishing, 2001), 165.

8. Thomas R. Kelly, *A Testament of Devotion* (New York: HarperCollins, 1941), 3.

9. Wiederkehr, *Angels*, 111.

11. Caring for Our Anger

1. Frederick Buechner, *Wishful Thinking: A Seeker's ABC*, rev. ed. (New York: HarperCollins, 1993), 2.

2. Big Book, 66.

3. Ibid., 64.

4. Thich Nhat Hanh, *Peace Is Every Step* (New York: Bantam Books, 1991), 57-58.

5. E. Glenn Hinson, "On Coping with Your Anger," *Weavings* 9, no. 2 (March–April 1994): 36.

6. Kurtz and Ketcham, *Spirituality of Imperfection* (see ch. 1, note 3), 217.

12. Granting and Accepting Forgiveness

1. John Mogabgab, "Editor's Introduction," *Weavings* 7, no. 2 (March–April 1992): 2.

2. Douglas V. Steere, *Dimensions of Prayer: Cultivating a Relationship with God*, rev. ed. (Nashville: Upper Room Books, 1997), 45-46.

3. Madeleine L'Engle, *The Weather of the Heart: Poems by Madeleine L'Engle* (Wheaton, IL: Harold Shaw Publishers, 1978), 84.

4. Marjorie J. Thompson, "Moving Toward Forgiveness," *Weavings* 7, no. 2 (March–April 1992): 19.

5. Allan Knight Chalmers, *High Wind at Noon: A Case for a Daring Christianity* (New York: Charles Scribner's Sons, 1948): 46-47.

6. Dag Hammarskjöld, *Markings* (New York: Alfred A. Knopf, 1964), 105.

13. Losing and Finding Faith in God

1. Wiederkehr, *Angels*, 49-50.

14. Saying Yes to God

1. Big Book, 152.

15. Surrender to Live

1. Big Book, 62.

2. Ibid.

3. Ibid., 60.

4. Ibid., 58.

5. Ibid., 63.

6. Dietrich Bonhoeffer, *The Cost of Discipleship* (New York: Simon & Schuster, 1959), 88.

7. Albert Einstein, *Ideas and Opinions* (New York: Random House, 1994), 12.

8. C. S. Lewis, *Mere Christianity* (New York: Macmillan Publishing Company, 1952), 114.

9. Karen Casey, *In God's Care: Daily Meditations on Spirituality in Recovery* (Center City, MN: Hazelden Foundation, 1991), 31.

10. Max Lucado, *Grace for the Moment: Inspirational Thoughts for Each Day of the Year* (Nashville: Thomas Nelson, 2000), 158.

11. Jean-Pierre de Caussade, *Abandonment to Divine Providence* (New York: Doubleday, 1975), passim.

12. Big Book, 60.

13. Thomas Merton, *Thoughts in Solitude* (New York: Farrar, Straus & Giroux, 1958), 79.